THE VEILED SUITE

THE VEILED SUITE

The Collected Poems

AGHA SHAHID ALI

W. W. NORTON & COMPANY

NEW YORK · LONDON

For information about permission to reproduce selections from this book,
write to Permissions, W. W. Norton & Company, Inc.,
500 Fifth Avenue, New York, NY 10110

For information about special discounts for bulk purchases, please contact
W. W. Norton Special Sales at specialsales@wwnorton.com or 800-233-4830

Manufacturing by Courier Westford
Book design by Chris Welch
Production manager: Devon Zahn

Library of Congress Cataloging-in-Publication Data

Agha, Shahid Ali, date.
The veiled suite : the collected poems of Agha Shahid Ali. — 1st ed.
p. cm.
Includes bibliographical references and index.
ISBN 978-0-393-06804-7
I. Title.
PR9499.3.A39V45 2009
821'.914—dc22

2008049968

W. W. Norton & Company, Inc.
500 Fifth Avenue, New York, N.Y. 10110
www.wwnorton.com

W. W. Norton & Company Ltd.
Castle House, 75/76 Wells Street, London W1T 3QT

1 2 3 4 5 6 7 8 9 0

CONTENTS

From   A WALK THROUGH THE
                 YELLOW PAGES

From THE COUNTRY WITHOUT
A POST OFFICE

From ◈ ROOMS ARE NEVER FINISHED

From CALL ME ISHMAEL TONIGHT

FOREWORD

gha Shahid Ali was, by his own count, the beneficiary of three cultures—Muslim, Hindu, and, for lack of a more precise rubric, Western. He grew up mostly in Srinagar, Kashmir, though the family lived for a few years in Indiana, where he attended high school. He often said that English was his first language and Urdu his mother tongue; however, throughout his life he wrote poetry only in English. His poems—like his conversation, for that matter—sounded like no one else's, no doubt because of the remarkable range and variety of his sources: the literatures of several continents; Bollywood, Hollywood, and art-house cinema; classical Indian and classical European music; and American pop. His later work in particular employs an unfashionable lavishness of diction and emotion, owing in equal measure, perhaps, to this extraordinary cultural inheritance, and an equally extraordinary generosity of spirit. (As a schoolmate once said of Gerard Manley Hopkins, "He gushes, but he means it.") There are cries of joy, despair, and grief that come off the page almost literally as cries.

Shahid's multiplicity of subject matter and reference poses a by now familiar problem, one that has been with us since high modernism, and particularly since the second half of the twentieth century, which saw a flourishing of—or, rather, a recognition of—hyphenated Englishes around the world. The dedicated reader has had no choice but to expand her range of reference as well. (And I can already hear the sound of scholars tapping away at their computers.) Islam exerts a particularly powerful gravitational force on many of these poems, which is yet another reason for non-Muslims to learn more about the faith. But for that matter, how many contemporary American readers of poetry possess the necessary theological apparatus to read *Four Quartets* unaided? Meanwhile, we might also console ourselves with the thought that certain great poems, and great poetries, are not incomprehensible, but *inexhaustible*; they reward rereading; they teach us and change us as we grow older with them.

However, I don't want to exaggerate this difficulty; the poems I refer to are found mostly in two of the later books, *The Country Without a Post Office* and *Rooms Are Never Finished*, both of which include useful notes that are reproduced here. And context itself is a help. By contrast, his "American" book, *A Nostalgist's Map of America*, is for the most part as wide open as the adopted country Shahid drove through while writing the poems. (He eventually became an American citizen in 2001.) Nor would a reader want to miss his light verse, for which he had a very deft touch. His chapbook, *A Walk Through the Yellow Pages*, contains half a dozen examples, including a few hilarious takes on the story of Little Red Riding Hood, parts of which, though, would have to be described as dark light verse.

When an interviewer asked Shahid about his philosophy, he replied, "I don't have a philosophy; I have a temperament." He might have said the same about his poetics. Though Shahid started out writing mostly in free verse, and then switched rather abruptly in mid-career to working in various demanding forms, he was never a partisan: he was willing to do whatever was necessary to put the poem across. But after *A Nostalgist's Map of America*, he began to feel that, for him, certain aspects of free verse had become "too easy," and he sensed the need for a new direction, new difficulties. His mother's illness and death, and a chance meeting with James Merrill—who no doubt would have said, "No accident!"—made the shift inevitable. His mother was diagnosed with brain cancer in 1996, which shook him to the core—years later he would say, repeatedly, "I can't believe that Mummy is dead." The pitch of grief in his poems about her is almost unbearable: such overwhelming emotion required new means. And Merrill's friendship and example encouraged him in every way; he even gave Shahid his first rhyming dictionary.

Shahid's memory was staggering—late in his life he memorized the whole of "Lycidas"—and he was a fearsome mimic. He had an ear cocked at all times for the surprising turn of phrase, the unintentional joke, the fresh bit of slang—anything that might be of use. He once overheard a woman say, while arguing with her husband, "Your memory keeps getting in the way of my history!" The line appears several times, with permutations, in "Farewell," in counterpoint with Tacitus's "They make a desolation and call it peace," as well as—a line of his own, I presume—"At a certain point I lost track of you." The magpie method is characteristic, as is the unexpected choice of form: the poem is written in monostichs, one-line stanzas. In fact Shahid made such daring choices as a matter of routine. His translations of the poems of Faiz Ahmed Faiz, collected in *The Rebel's Silhouette*, are entirely in free verse; given the stringencies of the ghazal, it may not be possible to achieve a translation that preserves the form. However, in a later translation of Faiz's ghazal, "Memory," Shahid chose to work the poem into Sapphic stanzas, of all things. It was an audaciously intuitive decision, to translate a ghazal—a Persian form that predates Chaucer—written in Urdu by a modern Pakistani poet, into an adaptation of a classical Greek stanza at least as unforgiving as the ghazal itself. The miracle is that the finished English poem is a heartbreaking masterpiece.

From the beginning Shahid's work included political poems—or what might more accurately be called poems about injustice.

However, as Allen Grossman said, "A poem is about something the way a cat is about the house." These poems are never mere essays on political matters, for what would be the point? The most vexing of these situations admit of no easy solutions, and besides, why would we expect a poet to be a political scientist as well? (However, Shahid did write a brilliant essay condemning the McCarran-Walter Act for a special issue of *Poetry East*.) He once sent Merrill a new poem about Bosnia, who wrote back at once, criticizing it for its weak rhymes. He said, "There's not much you can do about Bosnia, but you can make this a better poem," the wisdom of which reverberated for years.

Nothing caused Shahid more pain and outrage than the troubles in his beloved Kashmir. A general uprising against Indian rule broke out in 1990, followed by extremely harsh repression by Indian forces, which continues to this day. To my mind the most poignant of Shahid's political poems is "Hans Christian Ostro," which was based on a report of a young Norwegian traveler in Kashmir who was taken hostage and killed by militants in 1995. Kashmiris the world over were traumatized by the news: after all, theirs is a culture in which generosity and hospitality are elevated to high moral principles. Much of the poem is oblique, but it ends with a particularly haunting image, perhaps of the Kashmiri people themselves mourning the young man's death:

> And draped in rain
> of the last monsoon-storm,
> a beggar, ears pressed to that metal cry,
> will keep waiting on a ghost-platform,
> holding back his tears, waving every train
> Good-bye and Good-bye.

In a grotesque coincidence, Shahid himself was diagnosed with brain cancer only a few years after his mother had died of the disease. I remember one afternoon, late in his illness, when his Brooklyn apartment was thronged as usual with family and friends, everyone eating and drinking and talking—always talking. From time to time he would ask, in his kind but now absent-minded way—by this time he was almost blind, and increasingly confused—whether everyone knew everyone else, whether any of us wanted something to eat or drink. It was the reflexiveness of Shahid's questions, of his concern for our happiness, that so moved me. (Again, the cultural imperative: he told me that one summer in Srinagar so many friends and relatives came to visit the family that they had to give over the entire house to them and take up residence elsewhere for the duration.)

As we didn't know then, or rather tried not to think about, Shahid would be dead in a matter of months. He had written his final poem, his third canzone, the title poem of this collection. Its epigraph is a line spoken by himself in a dream, after his diagnosis: "Faceless, he could represent only two alternatives: that he was either a conscious agent of harm, or that he would unwittingly harm me anyway." Even the rationalists among us found the news of this visitation disturbing. Shahid died in Amherst, Massachusetts, on December 8, 2001. And now he has become not his admirers so much as his poems—or his world has become a book, as Mallarmé said it must. As Shahid himself would be the first to say, Welcome to it.

—Daniel Hall, Amherst, 2008

THE VEILED SUITE

The Veiled Suite

Faceless, he could represent only two alternatives:
that he was either a conscious agent of harm,
or that he would unknowingly harm me anyway. *

"No mortal has or will ever lift my veil,"
he says. Strokes my arm. What poison is his eyes?
Make me now your veil, then see if you can veil
yourself from me. Where is he not from? Which vale
of tears? Am I awake? There is little sense
of whether I am his — or he is my — veil.
For, after the night is fog, who'll unveil
whom? Either he knows he is one with the night
or is unaware he's an agent of night —
nothing else is possible (who is whose veil?)
when he, random assassin sent by the sea,
is putting, and with no sense of urgency,

the final touches on — whose last fantasy?
Where isn't he from? He's brought the sky from Vail,
Colorado, and the Ganges from Varanasi
in a clay urn (his heart measures like the sea).
He's brought the desert too. It's deep in his eyes
when he says: "I want you to be mine alone, see."
What hasn't he planned? For music Debussy,
then a song from New Orleans in the *Crescent's*
time nearing Penn Station. What's of the essence?
Not time, not time, no, not time. I can foresee
he will lead each night from night into night.
I ask, "Can you promise me this much tonight:

* From a dream in which I said this to myself (Spring 2000).

that when you divide what remains of this night
it will be like a prophet once parted the sea.
But no one must die! For however this night
has been summoned, I, your mortal every night,
must become your veil . . . and I must lift your veil
when just one thing's left to consider: the night."
There's just one thing left to consider, the night
in which we will be left to realize
when the ice begins to break down in his eyes.
And the prophecies filming his gaze tonight?
What will be revealed? What stunning color sense
kept hidden so long in his eyes, what essence

of longing? He can kill me without a license.
The moon for its ivory scours the night.
Sent by the fog, he nearly empties in me all sense
of his gaze, till either he or I have lost all sense;
midnight polishes the remains of a galaxy.
What is left to polish now? What fluorescence?
Is there some hope of making a world of sense?
When I meet his gaze, there is again the veil.
On the farthest side of prophecy, I still need a veil.
Perhaps our only chance will be to ignite
the doom he sometimes veils in his eyes,
and the universe lost, like I am, in his eyes.

I wait for him to look straight into my eyes.
This is our only chance for magnificence.
If he, carefully, upon this hour of ice,
will let us almost completely crystallize,
tell me, who but I could chill his dreaming night.
Where he turns, what will not appear but my eyes?
Wherever he looks, the sky is only eyes.
Whatever news he has, it is of the sea.
But now is the time when I am to realize
our night cannot end completely with his eyes.
Something has happened now for me to prevail,
no matter what remains of this final night.

What arrangements haven't you made for tonight!
I am to hand you a knife from behind the veil
now rising quickly from your just-lit incense.
I'm still alive, alive to learn from your eyes
that I am become your veil and I am all you see.

(for Patricia O'Neill)

THE HALF-INCH
HIMALAYAS

Postcard from Kashmir

Kashmir shrinks into my mailbox,
my home a neat four by six inches.

I always loved neatness. Now I hold
the half-inch Himalayas in my hand.

This is home. And this the closest
I'll ever be to home. When I return,
the colors won't be so brilliant,
the Jhelum's waters so clean,
so ultramarine. My love
so overexposed.

And my memory will be a little
out of focus, in it
a giant negative, black
and white, still undeveloped.

(for Pavan Sahgal)

A Lost Memory of Delhi

I am not born
it is 1948 and the bus turns
onto a road without name

There on his bicycle
my father
He is younger than I

At Okhla where I get off
I pass my parents
strolling by the Jamuna River

My mother is a recent bride
her sari a blaze of brocade
Silverdust parts her hair

She doesn't see me
The bells of her anklets are distant
like the sound of china from

teashops being lit up with lanterns
and the stars are coming out
ringing with tongues of glass

They go into the house
always faded in photographs
in the family album

but lit up now
with the oil lamp
I saw broken in the attic

I want to tell them I am their son
older much older than they are
I knock keep knocking

but for them the night is quiet
this the night of my being
They don't they won't

hear me they won't hear
my knocking drowning out
the tongues of stars

A Dream of Glass Bangles

Those autumns my parents slept
warm in a quilt studded
with pieces of mirrors

On my mother's arms were bangles
like waves of frozen rivers
and at night

after the prayers
as she went down to her room
I heard the faint sound of ice

breaking on the staircase
breaking years later
into winter

our house surrounded by men
pulling icicles for torches
off the roofs

rubbing them on the walls
till the cement's darkening red
set the tips of water on fire

the air a quicksand of snow
as my father stepped out
and my mother

inside the burning house
a widow smashing the rivers
on her arms

Snowmen

My ancestor, a man
of Himalayan snow,
came to Kashmir from Samarkand,
carrying a bag
of whale bones:
heirlooms from sea funerals.
His skeleton
carved from glaciers, his breath
arctic,
he froze women in his embrace.
His wife thawed into stony water,
her old age a clear
evaporation.

This heirloom,
his skeleton under my skin, passed
from son to grandson,
generations of snowmen on my back.
They tap every year on my window,
their voices hushed to ice.

No, they won't let me out of winter,
and I've promised myself,
even if I'm the last snowman,
that I'll ride into spring
on their melting shoulders.

Cracked Portraits

My grandfather's painted grandfather,
son of Ali, a strange physician
in embroidered robes, a white turban,
the Koran lying open on a table beside him.

I look for prayers
in his eyes, for inscriptions
in Arabic.
I find his will:
He's left us plots
in the family graveyard.

. . .

Great-grandfather? A sahib in breeches.
He simply disappoints me,
his hands missing in the drawing-room photo
but firm as he whipped the horses
or the servants.

He wound the gramophone to a fury,
the needles grazing Malika Pukhraj's songs
as he, drunk, tore his shirts
and wept at the refrain,
"I still am young."

. . .

Grandfather, a handsome boy,
sauntered toward madness
into Srinagar's interior.
In a dim-lit shop he smoked hashish,
reciting verses of Sufi mystics.
My father went to bring him home.

As he grew older, he moved toward Plato,
mumbling "philosopher-king,"

Napoleon on his lips.
Sitting in the bedroom corner,
smoking his hookah, he told me
the Siberian snows
froze the French bones.

In his cup,
Socrates swirled.

. . .

I turn the pages,
see my father holding a tennis racquet,
ready to score with women,
brilliance clinging to his shirt.

He brings me closer to myself
as he quotes Lenin's love of Beethoven,
but loses me as he turns to Gandhi.

Silverfish have eaten his boyhood face.

. . .

Cobwebs cling
to the soundless
words of my ancestors.

No one now comes from Kandahar,
dear Ali, to pitch tents by the Jhelum,
under autumn maples,
and claim descent from the holy prophet.

Your portrait is desolate
in a creaking corridor.

(for Agha Zafar Ali)

Story of a Silence

                While her husband
thumbed through Plato, spending
the dialogues

                like a pension,
in whispers, his inheritance lost,
his house

                taken away,
my gandmother worked hard, harder
than a man

                to earn
her salary from the government and
deserve

                her heirloom
of prayer from God. When he slept,
she leafed

                through
his dreams: she wasn't in any
of them

                and he
was just lying on the river's warm
glass, thousands

                    of him
moving under him. He was nothing
when he woke,

                    only his own
duplicates in her arms. Years later
she went

                    into the night,
in one hand the Koran, in the other
a minaret

                    of fire. She
found him sleeping, his torn Plato, his
pillow, the fire's

                    light a cold
quilt on him. She held him as only
a shadow must

                    be held. But
then the darkness cracked, and
he was gone.

Prayer Rug

Those intervals
between the day's
five calls to prayer

the women of the house
pulling thick threads
through vegetables

rosaries of ginger
of rustling peppers
in autumn drying for winter

in those intervals this rug
part of Grandma's dowry
folded

so the Devil's shadow
would not desecrate
Mecca scarlet-woven

with minarets of gold
but then the sunset
call to prayer

the servants
their straw mats unrolled
praying or in the garden

in summer on grass
the children wanting
the prayers to end

the women's foreheads
touching Abraham's
silk stone of sacrifice

black stone descended
from Heaven
the pilgrims in white circling it

this year my grandmother
also a pilgrim
in Mecca she weeps

as the stone is unveiled
she weeps holding on
to the pillars

(for Begum Zafar Ali)

The Dacca Gauzes

. . . for a whole year he sought
to accumulate the most exquisite
Dacca gauzes.
    —OSCAR WILDE, The Picture of Dorian Gray

Those transparent Dacca gauzes
known as woven air, running
water, evening dew:

a dead art now, dead over
a hundred years. "No one
now knows," my grandmother says,

"what it was to wear
or touch that cloth." She wore
it once, an heirloom sari from

her mother's dowry, proved
genuine when it was pulled, all
six yards, through a ring.

Years later when it tore,
many handkerchiefs embroidered
with gold-thread paisleys

were distributed among
the nieces and daughters-in-law.
Those too now lost.

In history we learned: the hands
of weavers were amputated,
the looms of Bengal silenced,

and the cotton shipped raw
by the British to England.
History of little use to her,

my grandmother just says
how the muslins of today
seem so coarse and that only

in autumn, should one wake up
at dawn to pray, can one
feel that same texture again.

One morning, she says, the air
was dew-starched: she pulled
it absently through her ring.

The Season of the Plains

In Kashmir, where the year
has four, clear seasons, my mother
spoke of her childhood

in the plains of Lucknow, and
of that season in itself,
the monsoon, when Krishna's

flute is heard on the shores
of the Jamuna. She played old records
of the Banaras thumri-singers,

Siddheshwari and Rasoolan, their
voices longing, when the clouds
gather, for that invisible

blue god. Separation
can't be borne when the rains
come: this every lyric says.

While children run out
into the alleys, soaking
their utter summer,

messages pass between lovers.
Heer and Ranjha and others
of legends, their love forbidden,

burned incense all night,
waiting for answers. My mother
hummed Heer's lament

but never told me if she
also burned sticks
of jasmine that, dying,

kept raising soft necks
of ash. I imagined
each neck leaning

on the humid air. She only
said: The monsoons never cross
the mountains into Kashmir.

A Monsoon Note on Old Age

This is fifty years later: I
sit across myself, folded in
monsoon sweat, my skin

shriveled, a tired eunuch, aware
only of an absence;
                              the window bars

sketch a prison on me;
                              I shuffle the stars,
a pack of old cards;

                              the night regains
its textures of rain. I overexpose
your photograph, dusting

death's far-off country.

A Butcher

In this lane
near Jama Masjid,*

where he wraps kilos of meat
in sheets of paper,

the ink of the news
stains his knuckles,

the script is wet
in his palms: Urdu,

bloody at his fingertips,
is still fine on his lips,

the language polished smooth
by knives

on knives. He hacks
the festival goats, throws

their skins to dogs.
I smile and quote

a Ghalib line; he completes
the couplet, smiles,

* Jama Masjid is the great mosque of Delhi. Ghalib and Mir, two of the greatest Urdu
poets, are especially known for their ghazals.

quotes a Mir line. I complete
the couplet.

He wraps my kilo of ribs.
I give him the money. The change

clutters our moment of courtesy,
our phrases snapping in mid-syllable,

Ghalib's ghazals left unrhymed.

The Fate of the Astrologer
Sitting on the Pavement Outside
the Delhi Railway Station

"Pay, pay attention to the sky,"
he shouts to passers-by.

The planets gather dust
from passing trucks.

After Seeing Kozintsev's *King Lear* in Delhi

Lear cries out "You are men of stones"
as Cordelia hangs from a broken wall.

I step out into Chandni Chowk, a street once
strewn with jasmine flowers
for the Empress and the royal women
who bought perfumes from Isfahan,
fabrics from Dacca, essence from Kabul,
glass bangles from Agra.

Beggars now live here in tombs
of unknown nobles and forgotten saints
while hawkers sell combs and mirrors
outside a Sikh temple. Across the street,
a theater is showing a Bombay spectacular.

I think of Zafar, poet and Emperor,
being led through this street
by British soldiers, his feet in chains,
to watch his sons hanged.

In exile he wrote:
"Unfortunate Zafar
spent half his life in hope,
the other half waiting.
He begs for two yards of Delhi for burial."

He was exiled to Burma, buried in Rangoon.

Chandni Chowk, Delhi

Swallow this summer street,
then wait for the monsoon.
Needles of rain

melt on the tongue. Will you go
farther? A memory of drought
holds you: you remember

the taste of hungry words
and you chew syllables of salt.

Can you rinse away this city that lasts
like blood on the bitten tongue?

Cremation

Your bones refused to burn
when we set fire to the flesh.

Who would have guessed
you'd be stubborn in death?

In Memory of Begum Akhtar

(d. 30 October 1974)

1

Your death in every paper,
boxed in the black and white
of photographs, obituaries,

the sky warm, blue, ordinary,
no hint of calamity,

no room for sobs,
even between the lines.

I wish to talk of the end of the world.

2

Do your fingers still scale the hungry
Bhairavi, or simply the muddy shroud?

Ghazal, that death-sustaining widow,
sobs in dingy archives, hooked to you.
She wears her grief, a moon-soaked white,
corners the sky into disbelief.

You've finally polished catastrophe,
the note you seasoned with decades
of Ghalib, Mir, Faiz:

I innovate on a noteless raga.

3

Exiling you to cold mud,
your coffin, stupid and white,
astounds by its ignorance.

It wears its blank pride,
defleshing the nomad's echo.
I follow you to the earth's claw,

shouldering time's shadow.
This is history's bitter arrogance,
this moment of the bone's freedom.

4

You cannot cross-examine the dead.

I've taken the circumstantial evidence,
your records, pictures, tapes, and
offered a careless testimony.

I wish to summon you in defense,
but the grave's damp and cold, now when
Malhar longs to stitch the rain,

wrap you in its notes: you elude
completely. The rain doesn't speak,
and life, once again, closes in,

reasserting this earth where the air
meets in a season of grief.

(for Saleem Kidwai)

Homage to Faiz Ahmed Faiz

(d. 20 November 1984)

*"You are welcome to make your
adaptations of my poems."*

1

You wrote this from Beirut, two years before
the Sabra-Shatila massacres. That city's
refugee air was open, torn
by jets and the voices of reporters.
As always, you were witness to "rains of stones,"

though you were away from Pakistan, from
the laws of home which said: the hands
of thieves will be surgically
amputated. But the subcontinent always spoke
to you: in Ghalib's Urdu, and sometimes through

the old masters who sang of twilight
but didn't live, like Ghalib, to see the wind
rip the collars of the dawn: the summer
of 1857, the trees of Delhi
became scaffolds: 30,000 men

were hanged. Wherever you were, Faiz, that
language spoke to you; and when you heard it,
you were alone —in Tunis, Beirut,
London, or Moscow. Those poets' laments
concealed, as yours revealed, the sorrows

of a broken time. You knew Ghalib was right:
blood must not merely follow routine, must not
just flow as the veins' uninterrupted
river. Sometimes it must flood the eyes,
surprise them by being clear as water.

2

I didn't listen when my father
recited your poems to us
by heart. What could it mean to a boy

that you had redefined the cruel
beloved, that figure who already
was Friend, Woman, God? In your hands

she was Revolution. You gave
her silver hands, her lips were red.
Impoverished lovers waited all

night every night, but she remained
only a glimpse behind
light. When I learned of her,

I was no longer a boy, and Urdu
a silhouette traced
by the voices of singers,

by Begum Akhtar, who wove your couplets
into ragas: both language and music
were sharpened. I listened:

and you became, like memory,
necessary. *Dast-e-Saba,*
I said to myself. And quietly

the wind opened its palms: I read
there of the night: the secrets
of lovers, the secrets of prisons.

3

When you permitted my hands to turn to stone,
as must happen to a translator's hands,

I thought of you writing *Zindan-Nama*
on prison walls, on cigarette packages,

on torn envelopes. Your lines were measured
so carefully to become in our veins

the blood of prisoners. In the free verse
of another language I imprisoned

each line — but I touched my own exile.
This hush, while your ghazals lay in my palms,

was accurate, as is this hush that falls
at news of your death over Pakistan

and India and over all of us no
longer there to whom you spoke in Urdu.

Twenty days before your death you finally
wrote, this time from Lahore, that after the sack

of Beirut you had no address . . . I
had gone from poem to poem, and found

you once, terribly alone, speaking
to yourself: "Bolt your doors, Sad heart! Put out

the candles, break all cups of wine. No one,
now no one will ever return." But you

still waited, Faiz, for that God, that Woman,
that Friend, that Revolution, to come

at last. And because you waited,
I listen as you pass with some song,

a memory of musk, the rebel face of hope.

A Wrong Turn

In my dream I'm always
in a massacred town, its name
erased from maps,
no road signs to it.
Only a wrong turn brings me here

where only the noon sun lives.
I'm alone, walking among the atrocities,
guillotines blood-scorched,
gods stabbed at their altars,
dry wells piled up with bones,
a curfew on ghosts.

Who were these people?
And who finished them to the last?
If dust had an alphabet, I would learn.

I thrust my hand
into the cobwebbed booth
of the town's ghost station,
the platform a snake-scaled rock,
rusted tracks waiting for a lost train,
my ticket a dead spider
hard as stone.

Vacating an Apartment

1

Efficient as Fate,
each eye a storm trooper,

the cleaners wipe my smile
with Comet fingers
and tear the plaster
off my suicide note.

They learn everything
from the walls' eloquent tongues.

Now, quick as genocide,
they powder my ghost for a cinnamon jar.

They burn my posters
(India and Heaven in flames),

whitewash my voicestains,

make everything new,
clean as Death.

2

When the landlord brings new tenants,
even Memory is a stranger.

The woman, her womb solid with the future,
instructs her husband's eyes
to clutch insurance policies.

They ignore my love affair with the furniture,
the corner table that memorized
my crossed-out lines.

Oh, she's beautiful,
a hard-nippled Madonna.

The landlord gives them my autopsy;
they sign the lease.

The room is beating with bottled infants,
and I've stopped beating.

I'm moving out holding tombstones in my hands.

The Previous Occupant

The landlady says he lived here
for years. There's enough missing
for me to know him. On the empty shelves,
absent books gather dust: Neruda. Cavafy.
I know he knew their poetry, by heart
the lines I love.

From a half-torn horoscope I learn
his sign: Aquarius, just like me.
A half-empty Flexsol in the cabinet:
he wore soft lenses. Yes, Aquarians are vain.
And no anthems on their lips, they travel
great distances. He came from some country
as far as Chile.

She says the apartment
will be cleaned by the 1st:

But no detergent will rub his voice from the air
though he has disappeared in some country
as far as Chile.
The stains of his thoughts still cling
in phrases to the frost on the windows.

And though he is blinded in some prison,
though he is dying in some country
as far as Chile,
no spray will get inside the mirror
from where his brown eyes,

brown, yes, brown,
stare as if for years he'd been
searching for me.

Now that he's found me,
my body casts his shadow everywhere.
He'll never, never, move out of here.

Leaving Your City

In the midnight bar
your breath collapsed on me.
I balanced on

the tip of your smile,

holding on to your words
as I climbed the dark steps.

Meticulous,
your furniture neatly arranged for death,

you sharpened the knife
on the moon's surface,
polished it with lunatic silver.

You were kind,
reciting poetry in a drunk tongue.
I thought: At last!

Now I loiter in and out
of your memory,

speaking to you wherever I go.

I'm reduced to my poverties

and you to a restless dream
from another country

where the sea is the most expensive blue.

. . .

My finger, your phone number
at its tip, dials the night.

And your city follows me,
its lights dying in my eyes.

Philadelphia, 2:00 A.M.

All routes to death
will open up, again,
as the bars close all over
Pennsylvania:

The disco stills its lights.
My eyes dim,
                then go off

in the mirrors;
                I swallow
the melting rocks in my glass,

looking for shortcuts
by-passing death,

my skin tense with
the taxi-hour of loss.

(for Howard Motyl)

The Jogger on Riverside Drive, 5:00 A.M.

The dark scissors of his legs
cut the moon's

raw silk, highways of wind
torn into lanes, his feet

pushing down the shadow
whose patterns he becomes

while trucks, one by one,
pass him by,

headlights pouring
from his face, his eyes

cracked as the Hudson
wraps street lamps

in its rippled blue shells,
the summer's thin, thin veins

bursting with dawn,
he, now suddenly free,

from the air, from himself,
his heart beating far, far

behind him.

Flight from Houston in January

Both sides of the sky
are visible from here,

the clouds below us
and a clear blue above.

If clouds were boats,
one would row them

with rods of lightning
across the world.

In Houston, already perhaps
a thousand miles back,

for days I saw the warm
side of the sky, the sun

touched with Mexico . . .

We drop through thousands
of feet of clouds,

the wings threshing them
like cotton for quilts.

Suddenly, the white hills
of Pittsburgh . . .

I see only the dark side
of the sky

as we hit the frozen runway.
A Pan Am takes off,

leaving behind
a row of snow dervishes

whirling and whirling
till they become the trance

of everwhite trees
found on Christmas cards . . .

The trees crumble, just
so much white dust.

Stationery

The moon did not become the sun.
It just fell on the desert
in great sheets, reams
of silver handmade by you.
The night is your cottage industry now,
the day is your brisk emporium.
The world is full of paper.

Write to me.

Survivor

Someone lives in my house

At night he opens the refrigerator
inhaling the summer's coriander

On Radio Kashmir he hears announced
all search has been abandoned
for last year's climbers
on Nanga Parbat

My house breaks
with the sympathy of neighbors

This is his moment

In my room
he sits at the table
practices my signature answers my mail

He wears the cardigan
my mother knit for my return

The mirror gives up
my face to him

He calls to my mother in my voice

She turns

He is breathless to tell her tales
in which I was never found

I Dream It Is Afternoon When
I Return to Delhi

At Purana Qila I am alone, waiting
for the bus to Daryaganj. I see it coming,
but my hands are empty.
"Jump on, jump on," someone shouts,
"I've saved this change for you
for years. Look!"
A hand opens, full of silver rupees.
"Jump on, jump on." The voice doesn't stop.
There's no one I know. A policeman,
handcuffs silver in his hands,
asks for my ticket.

I jump off the running bus,
sweat pouring from my hair.
I run past the Doll Museum, past
headlines on the Times of India
building, PRISONERS BLINDED IN A BIHAR
JAIL, HARIJAN VILLAGES BURNED BY LANDLORDS.
Panting, I stop in Daryaganj,
outside Golcha Cinema.

Sunil is there, lighting
a cigarette, smiling. I say,
"It must be ten years, you haven't changed,
it was your voice on the bus!"
He says, "The film is about to begin,
I've bought an extra ticket for you,"
and we rush inside:

Anarkali is being led away,
her earrings lying on the marble floor.
Any moment she'll be buried alive.
"But this is the end," I turn
toward Sunil. He is nowhere.
The usher taps my shoulder, says
my ticket is ten years old.

Once again my hands are empty.
I am waiting, alone, at Purana Qila.
Bus after empty bus is not stopping.
Suddenly, beggar women with children
are everywhere, offering
me money, weeping for me.

A Call

I close my eyes. It doesn't leave me,
the cold moon of Kashmir which breaks
into my house

and steals my parents' love.

                   I open my hands:
empty, empty. This cry is foreign.

"When will you come home?"
Father asks, then asks again.

The ocean moves into the wires.

I shout, "Are you all happy?"
The line goes dead.

The waters leave the wires.

The sea is quiet, and over it
the cold, full moon of Kashmir.

The Tiger at 4:00 A.M.

Something waits
to print on this blankness,

something still asleep
in an envelope of fur,

outside in the January snow.
I open the window:

On the slopes of Kumaon
ten thousand miles away,

in terror of the man-eater,
the peasants lock themselves in,

their huts wrapped
in a plaster of frost.

On the table before me,
the wind rustles the page.

Something begins to stir:

The villagers are coming
back to life,

the sun once again
dresses their huts.

It soaks up the dawn's
washable blues.

Something stalks through the page.

In the Mountains

Somewhere
without me
my life begins

He who lives it
counts on a cold rosary
God's ninety-nine Names in Arabic

The unknown hundredth he finds in glaciers
then descends into wet saffron fields
where I wait to hold him

but wrapped in ice
he by-passes me
in his phantom cart

He lets go of the hundredth Name
which rises in calligraphy from his palm
Fog washes the sudden skeletons of maples

Farther into the year by a broken fireplace
I clutch the shiver of a last flame
and forget every Name of God

And there in the mountains
the Koran frozen to his fingertips
he waits

farther much farther into the year
he waits for news of my death

Houses

The man who buries his house in the sand
and digs it up again, each evening,
learns to put it together quickly

and just as quickly to take it apart.
My parents sleep like children in the dark.
I am too far to hear them breathe

but I remember their house is safe
and I can sleep, the night's hair
black and thick in my hands.

My parents sleep in the dark.
When the moon rises, the night's hair
turns white in my arms.

I am thirteen thousand miles from home.
I comb the moon out of the night,
and my parents are sleeping like children.

"My father is dead," Vidur writes,
and a house in my neighborhood, next
to my parents', has burned down.

I keep reading the letter.
                    If I wake up,
my body will be water, reflecting the fire.

(for Jon Anderson)

A WALK THROUGH
THE YELLOW PAGES

Bell Telephone Hours

1.
Has anyone heard from you
lately?

The living . . . only the living,
their area codes once
visible in their eyes.
I flipped through their visions,
left my number in their sleep.
But no one called back.
I called all night,
called for years,
called till their lids began to ring,
ten, twenty, two hundred times,
and then they went blind
on my dreams.
Now their eyes don't open.
No one picks up the phone.
I only hear
the busy signals
of their nightmares.

2.
Call long distance: the next
best thing to being there.

The rich . . . forever
on my list
of frequently called numbers
took long expensive vacations.
My long distance Annoyance Calls
were heavily fined,
my breath was disconnected.
When I breathed again,
my fingers walked
through the yellow pages.

Then I mailed my bones
wrapped in bare dreams.
Courteous, I enclosed
a stamped envelope.
But no one answered.

Directory Assistance,
give me the magic number
for Necropolis, U.S.A.

3.
It's getting late. Do your
friends know where you are?

They know my debts are unpaid,
they won't look for me. But
if they call, say I'm at the phone booth,
talking long distance to the dead.
This is the longest distance
I've called. And the bill is running up.

Before I run out of change,
I must report:
The cremations aren't working,
someone's left the bones off their hooks.

Operator,
I'm still getting busy signals.

4.
Reach out and touch someone
far away. Use your phone
for all it's worth.

Once I plugged into the sleep of friends
and interrupted their dreams.
I spent years apologizing.
Once I let the phone ring
till the dead woke up.
They told me they were sick of the earth.
They told me to dial the sea.

"Underground Line Locating Service,
get me the sea when there's no ice,
when the water is pure, absolutely
free." I've lost faith in half-rates.

5.
Today, talk is cheap.
Call somebody.

I called Information Desk, Heaven,
and asked, "When is Doomsday?"
I was put on hold.

Through the hallelujahs of seraphs,
I heard the idle gossip of angels,
their wings beating rumours
of revolts in Heaven.
Then I heard flames, wings burning,
then only hallelujahs.

I prayed, "Angel of Love,
please pick up the phone."

But it was the Angel of Death.
I said, "Tell me, Tell me,
when is Doomsday?"

He answered, "God is busy.
He never answers the living.
He has no answers for the dead.
Don't ever call again collect."

Advertisement (Found Poem)

CANTON the oriental food store
carries DIM SUMS
those Chinese pastries Buns Dumplings and all
kinds of delicacies

In States you can taste them
only in Chinatown tea house

With a cup of tea
you can take DIM SUMS

                         as breakfast
                         as lunch
                         as brunch or
                         as snack

It is most delightful
to serve DIM SUMS
in a party too

DIM SUMS are different to instant noodles
or instant soups
Our DIM SUMS are freshly frozen food

AND need only 15 minutes of steaming to eat

Simply 15 minutes
no work no greasy mess

Buy from CANTON
DIM SUMS
and Try

Language Games

I went mad in your house of words,
purposely mad, so you would
give me asylum.

I went mad to undergo
a therapy of syllables.

But you prescribed crosswords,
anagrams for sleeping pills.
That didn't work.

You bought a Scrabble game.
I juggled the white pieces,
maybe a hundred times.
But my seven letters
were all vowels.

When you spoke again,
my sorrow turned deaf:
I couldn't hear you smile.

. . .

Words never evade you,
you can build anything.

You can build a whole hour
with only seven seconds.

Framed with consonants,
we resumed play, no vowels
in my seven letters.
I saw you do wonders without vowels.

Let's give up, I said,
but you cried: Truth AND Consequences!
I rocked shut to sounds.

You challenged me to Charades.
I agreed. This
would be my syllable-cure.

Tableau One: I licked a saucer of milk.
You cried: CAT!
Tableau Two: I was stubborn as a mule.
You cried: ASS!
Tableau Three: I gave you my smile, like a prize.
You cried: TROPHY!

You cried: CAT-ASS-TROPHY?
You cried: CATASTROPHE!

And I lost.
No chance of you insane.

And I wanted you mad
so I could cure you.

Please,
Please go mad,
so I can build you an asylum.

Poets on Bathroom Walls

Sipping our Miller Lites, you
announce you must take a break.
So you're off, dear girl, to those
remote regions where women do
sitting what I do standing.

You come back,
having memorized someone's graffiti:

"It's evident to all the world
that I'm alone. My lips are still
glistening at the end of the day."

And the answer someone's scrawled in red:

"Spies have sanctioned evidence of your sorrow.
I've never met you
despite all the world."

Having returned with nothing from the Men's Room,
I tell you I want those two women to meet.
I want them to meet,
despite all the world.

(for Nancy McGartland)

Christmas, 1980s

In America
it is also the season of suicides

The trees light up red in shop-windows
What I touch is charged with voltage

I hear the lethal carols
as I make contacts
among Hell's Angels

I walk rapidly
back to my house
and lock the door

I lift the phone

I dial a joke
I don't laugh

I call Cops for Christ
I call Murder, Inc.
I call Reverend Moon

I make an obscene call
to the White House

I light a candle in my window
brief for any doomed republic

the flame out

An Interview with Red Riding Hood, Now No Longer Little

"How dark it was inside the wolf!"
—RED RIDING HOOD in the Grimms' tale

Q. Whatever happened after
    the wolf died?

A. My father, a self-made man,
    he made good.
    Mind you, no ordinary woodsman,
    he slowly bought the whole forest,
    had it combed for wolves.
    Had it cut down.
    But the wolves escaped,
    like guerillas, into
    the mountains.
    He owns a timber industry.
    I, of course, am an heiress.

Q. And your grandma?

A. She had nightmares.
    She'd wake up crying, "Wolf! Wolf!"
    We had to put her in a home.
    I took her baskets of fruit,
    flowers, cakes, wines.
    Always in the red velvet cap.
    I got sick of lisping for her,
    "Grandma, what big eyes you have!"
    That always made her laugh.
    The last time I saw her, she cried,
    "Save me, he's coming to eat me up!"
    We gave her a quiet burial.

Q. Do you have any regrets?

A. Yes.
   I lied when I said it was dark.
   Now I drive through the city,
   hearing wolves at every turn.
   How warm it was inside the wolf!

The Wolf's Postscript to
"Little Red Riding Hood"

First, grant me my sense of history:
I did it for posterity,
for kindergarten teachers
and a clear moral:
Little girls shouldn't wander off
in search of strange flowers,
and they mustn't speak to strangers.

And then grant me my generous sense of plot:
Couldn't I have gobbled her up
right there in the jungle?
Why did I ask her where her grandma lived?
As if I, a forest-dweller,
didn't know of the cottage
under the three oak trees
and the old woman who lived there
all alone?
As if I couldn't have swallowed her years before?

And you may call me the Big Bad Wolf,
now my only reputation.
But I was no child-molester
though you'll agree she was pretty.

And the huntsman:
Was I sleeping while he snipped
my thick black fur
and filled me with garbage and stones?
I ran with that weight and fell down,
simply so children could laugh
at the noise of the stones
cutting through my belly,
at the garbage spilling out
with a perfect sense of timing,
just when the tale
should have come to an end.

Hansel's Game

In those years I lived
happily ever after. And still do.
I played with every Gretel in town
including Gretel, my sister.

I walked into the forest,
trailing moon-sharpened pebbles
and traced back a route
from the grave to the womb.

Such stories end happily,
Mother said.

Darling, go out into the world,
the womb's no place for a big boy like you.

I wouldn't, I wouldn't.
She pushed
but I stuck on like gum.

So she baked garlic bread,
she knew I loved it.
And I dropped like a coin
once again into the world.

And again I walked into the forest,
lost in toadstools, thickets, ferns, and thorn,
and Gretel was hungry,

but I threw the bread,
crumb by crumb,
to light my route
from the womb to the grave.

When the moon rose,
the crumbs were gone.
A witch had to be somewhere near.

Well, I knew the ending,
I knew she would end badly,
a big boy now, I knew what witches do:
They drain big boys and ice them
with almonds and thick chocolate.

I didn't let her, I played innocent.

And Gretel and I lived
happily ever after. And still do:

We have a big ice-box
in our basement
where we keep the witch.

Now and then we take portions of her
to serve on special occasions.

And our old father washes
her blood from the dishes.

A NOSTALGIST'S MAP
OF AMERICA

Eurydice

I am a woman
brought limping to Hell

under the Night
and Fog decree.

But they've let him come
here to Belsen, rare passenger

in a river-green van,
ferried in by an old chauffeur

who drives past
the howl-choked dogs

at the fence. At a shudder
of coals, trains unload

wide-eyed children,
who now flock around him.

Yes, he is here,
he who, people said,

could dissolve bombs
in mid-air

when he played Beethoven.
Now the guards weep

as he begins
his own Dream of Calliope.

The smoke hangs down its arms
over the chimneys,

clearing the ghost-washed air.
Yes, I will soon be

on the train with him,
rushing along the upper Rhine.

But a guard hands him papers,
he has done something, no,

he must not do something,
he leafs

through the papers,
he must not, what?

He is pushed into the van.
His gaze runs through my tears,

stringing them into a necklace
that chokes me

as my farewell
amplifies in a sudden

tunnel of mustard twilight.

Beyond the Ash Rains

What have you known of loss
That makes you different from other men?
— Gilgamesh

When the desert refused my history,
refused to acknowledge that I had lived
there, with you, among a vanished tribe,

two, three thousand years ago, you parted
the dawn rain, its thickest monsoon curtains,

and beckoned me to the northern canyons.
There, among the red rocks, you lived alone.
I had still not learned the style of nomads:

to walk between the rain drops to keep dry.
Wet and cold, I spoke like a poor man,

without irony. You showed me the relics
of our former life, proof that we'd at last
found each other, but in your arms I felt

singled out for loss. When you lit the fire
and poured the wine, "I am going," I murmured,

repeatedly, "going where no one has been
and no one will be. . . . Will you come with me?"
You took my hand, and we walked through the streets

of an emptied world, vulnerable
to our suddenly bare history in which I was,

but you said won't again be, singled
out for loss in your arms, won't ever again
be exiled, never again, from your arms.

A Rehearsal of Loss

The night rose from the rocks of the canyon.

I drove away from your door. And the night,
it left the earth the way a broken man,

his lover's door closing behind him, leaves
that street in silence for the rest of his life.

Crucifixion

Among the Penitentes in New Mexico — just
before Easter — there is a flurry of marriages.

You who are driving clear of memory,
north from Las Cruces, and far from yourself,
and farther, past dunes of whitest gypsum,
past the rock that once sprouted wings and bore
the besieged Navajos to safety, past

the timbered forests the Penitentes haunt
(nomads of the Sangre de Cristos who
crucify, each Easter, one of their own),
don't know as you're climbing higher, alone,
so terribly alone, and the blue pines

are like men, descending from the summits,
that a virgin bachelor has been chosen,
that, as the road whitens in the moonlight,
a cross is being built in a secret hut:
and as braided ropes of yucca fibers

are soaked in streams, you don't know that Silence,
answered by its own echo from every
direction, is at that moment turning
all history to flesh — so that you will
again be filled with sorrow, and a god,

suddenly more mortal than any man,
will return to his sanctuary to find
just life, with no escapes, his idol smashed,
the bones of his last worshipers on earth
scattered everywhere, no one left to hear

his secret weeping: and when memory,
in the grief of broken stone, is nothing
but flesh, you will hear Silence—as it was
once answered by someone running, a god
escaping, his skin the color of sky

so that his sweat, wherever he caught his breath,
seeped into underground caves and hardened
into turquoise: and as you leave the hills,
washed now neither of memory nor pain,
the gods will have already happened

and you will know it is too late, always
too late (for whose world is not in ruins?
whose?), that he won't be saved, that bachelor,
lashed with ropes soaked in water, blood running
down his back as through the timbered forests

he carries the cross, and you, much farther
from yourself, will know his sandals have been
left outside his parents' door and his grave
in a secret cave of turquoise will not
be revealed for a year: and you, driving

faster now, will know that a son won't be
returning, never coming home, and when
far behind you the dawn is blood, the sky
a final altar, you will see the trees
once again as men, ascending the hills.

(for Christopher Merrill)

Leaving Sonora

living in the desert
has taught me to go inside myself
for shade
—RICHARD SHELTON

Certain landscapes insist on fidelity.
Why else would a poet of this desert
go deep inside himself for shade?
Only there do the perished tribes live.
The desert insists, always: Be faithful,
even to those who no longer exist.

The Hohokam lived here for 1500 years.
In his shade, the poet sees one of their women,
beautiful, her voice low as summer thunder.
Each night she saw, among the culinary ashes,
what the earth does only through a terrible pressure—
the fire, in minutes, transforming the coal into diamonds.

I left the desert at night—to return
to the East. From the plane I saw Tucson's lights
shatter into blue diamonds. My eyes dazzled
as we climbed higher: below a thin cloud,
and only for a moment, I saw those blue lights fade
into the outlines of a vanished village.

I Dream I Return to Tucson in the Monsoons

and the streets light up
with the afternoon sun
I remember when I was alone
There was only the rain

At Gates Pass I walk up to the rocks
pieces of blue glass scattered everywhere
I remember when there was nothing but the rain
I remember when there was nothing but the silence
There was only the desert below

The moon touched my shoulder
and I longed for a vanished love

The moon turned the desert to water

For a moment I saw islands
as they began to sink

The ocean was a dried floor

Below me is a world without footprints
I am alone I'm still alone
and there's no trace anywhere of the drowned

The sun is setting over
what was once an ocean

A Nostalgist's Map of America

A Route of Evanescene
With a revolving Wheel —
A Resonance of Emerald —
A Rush of Cochineal —
And every Blossom on the Bush
Adjusts its tumbled Head —
The mail from Tunis, probably,
An easy Morning's Ride —
—EMILY DICKINSON

The trees were soon hushed in the resonance
of darkest emerald as we rushed by
on 322, that route which took us from
the dead center of Pennsylvania.

(a stone marks it) to a suburb ten miles
from Philadelphia. "A hummingbird,"
I said, after a sharp turn, then pointed
to the wheel, still revolving in your hand.

I gave Emily Dickinson to you then,
line after line, complete from heart. The signs
on Schuylkill Expressway fell neat behind us.
I went further: "Let's pretend your city

is Evanescence — There has to be one —
in Pennsylvania — And that some day —
the Bird will carry — my letters — to you —
from Tunis — or Casablanca — the mail

an easy night's ride — from North Africa."
I'm making this up, I know, but since you
were there, none of it's a lie. How did I
go on? "Wings will rush by when the exit

to Evanescence is barely a mile?"
The sky was dark teal, the moon was rising.
"It always rains on this route," I went on,
"which takes you back, back to Evanescence,

your boyhood town." You said *this* was summer,
this final end of school, this coming home
to Philadelphia, WMMR
as soon as you could catch it. What song first

came on? It must have been a disco hit,
one whose singer no one recalls. It's six,
perhaps seven years since then, since you last
wrote. And yesterday when you phoned, I said,

"I knew you'd call," even before you could
say who you were. "I am in Irvine now
with my lover, just an hour from Tuscon,
and the flights are cheap." "Then we'll meet often."

For a moment you were silent, and then,
"Shahid, I'm dying." I kept speaking to you
after I hung up, my voice the quickest
mail, a cracked disc with many endings,

each false: One: "I live in Evanescence
(I had to build it, for America
was without one). All is safe here with me.
Come to my street, disguised in the climate

of Southern California. Surprise
me when I open the door. Unload skies
of rain from your distance-drenched arms." Or this:
"Here in Evanescence (which I found—though

not in Pennsylvania—after I last
wrote), the eavesdropping willows write brief notes
on grass, then hide them in shadows of trunks.
I'd love to see you. Come as you are." And

this, the least false: "You said each month you need
new blood. Please forgive me, Phil, but I thought
of your pain as a formal feeling, one
useful for the letting go, your transfusions

mere wings to me, the push of numerous
hummingbirds, souvenirs of Evanescence
seen disappearing down a route of veins
in an electric rush of cochineal."

(for Philip Paul Orlando)

In Search of Evanescence

"It was a year of brilliant water."
—THOMAS DE QUINCEY

1

Students of mist
climbing the stairs like dust
washing history off the shelves
will never know this house never
that professors here in glass sneakers
used window squares for crosswords
moving the weather from sky to sky
under their arms new editions of water

while mirrors left lying on coffee tables
tore the glare from the windows
and glued vanishing rainbows
to the walls the ceilings

will never know the sun's quick reprints

2

It was a year of brilliant water
in Pennsylvania that final summer
seven years ago, the sun's quick reprints

in my attaché case: those students
of mist have drenched me with dew, I'm driving
away from that widow's house, my eyes open

to a dream of drowning. But even
when I pass—in Ohio—the one exit
to Calcutta, I don't know I've begun

mapping America, the city limits
of Evanescence now everywhere. It
was a year of brilliant water, Phil,

such a cadence of dead seas at each turn:
so much refused to breathe in those painted
reflections, trapped there in ripples of hills:

a woman climbed the steps to Acoma,
vanished into the sky. In the ghost towns
of Arizona, there were charcoal tribes

with desert voices, among their faces
always the last speaker of a language.
And there was always thirst: a train taking me

from Bisbee, that copper landscape with bones,
into a twilight with no water. Phil,
I never told you where I'd been these years,

swearing fidelity to anyone.
Now there's only regret: I didn't send you
my routes of Evanescence. You never wrote.

3

When on Route 80 in Ohio
I came across an exit
to Calcutta

the temptation to write a poem
led me past the exit
so I could say

India always exists
off the turnpikes
of America

so I could say
I did take the exit
and crossed Howrah

and even mention the Ganges
as it continued its sobbing
under the bridge

so when I paid my toll
I saw trains rush by
one after one

on their roofs old passengers
each ready to surrender
his bones for tickets

so that I heard
the sun's percussion
on tamarind leaves

heard the empty cans of children
filling only with the shadows
of leaves

that behind the unloading trucks
were the voices of vendors
bargaining over women

so when the trees
let down their tresses
the monsoon oiled and braided them

and when the wind again parted them
this was the temptation
to end the poem this way:

The warm rains have left
many dead on the pavements

The signs to Route 80
all have disappeared

And now the road is a river
polished silver by cars

The cars are urns
carrying ashes to the sea

4

Someone wants me to live   A language will die with me

                    (once
spoken by proud tribesmen
in the canyons east
of the Catalinas   or much farther north

in the Superstition Mountains)   It will die with me

(Someone wants me to live)

It has the richest consonants   exact
for any cluster of sorrows

that haunt the survivors of Dispersal   that country
which has no map

but it has histories   most
of them forgotten
scraps of folklore   (once

in mountains   there were silver cities
with flags   on every rooftop
on each flag a prayer   read

by the wind   a passer-by forgiven all
when the wind became his shirt)

Someone wants me to live
so he can learn

those prayers
that language   he is asking me
questions

He wants me to live

and as I speak he is freezing
my words   he will melt them
years later

to listen   and listen
to the water   of my voice

when he is the last
speaker of his language

5

From the Faraway Nearby—
of Georgia O'Keeffe—these words—
Black Iris—Dark Iris—Abstraction, Blue—
her hands—around—a skull—

"The plains—the wonderful—
great big sky—makes me—
want to breathe—so deep—
that I'll break—"

From her Train—at Night—in the Desert—
I its only—passenger—
I see—as they pass by—her red hills—
black petals—landscapes with skulls—

"There is—so much—of it—
I want to get outside—of it all—
I would—if I could—
even if it killed me—"

6

"I have no house, only a shadow."
—MALCOLM LOWRY

In Pennsylvania seven years ago,
it was a year of brilliant water,
a resonance of oceans at each turn.

It's again that summer, Phil, and the end
of that summer again: you are driving
toward the Atlantic, drowning in my

brilliant dream of water. I too am leaving,
the sun's reprints mine. There are red hills
at the end of my drive through three thousand

miles of Abstraction, Blue—the Blue that will
always be here after all destruction
is finished. "Phil was afraid of being

forgotten." But it's again a year of water,
and in a house always brilliant with lights
I'm saying to a stranger what I should

have said to you: "I have no house only
a shadow but whenever you are in need
of a shadow my shadow is yours."

7

We must always have a place
to store the darkness

but in your house all the lights are on
even during the day

The fluorescents you say
are like detergent
They whitewash the walls and the ceilings

Your vacuum sucks in half-shadows
from your carpets

and as you climb the stairs
the wax polishes the sound of your footsteps

What can I be but a stranger in your house?

My house is damp with decades in which
the sun was dark

I keep all my lights off
During the day I shut the blinds

No
Don't even bring a candle when you come

8

You
sometimes suddenly
the son I'll never have

Mediterranean boy
Icarus of the night

You drive your car
its wheels dying
on the platinum tar of tides
a highway on the sea
paved by the rising moon

Sirens whispering
on their lips the sinking
breaths of salt

whispering from Istanbul to Tunis
whispering their silver fractures
at the booths where your hand
rich with planets for coins
pays toll

your windows rolled down
the brine pouring its green change
into your car

9

"I want to eat Evanescence slowly."
—EMILY DICKINSON

The way she had—in her rushes—of resonance—
I too—so want to eat—Evanescence—slowly—

in the near—faraways—of the heart. Like O'Keeffe
also—in her Faraway Nearby—that painting,

this ghost-station—from where her Train—in the Desert—
at Night—will depart—its passenger—only I—

banished to the soul—of the desert—from its heart.
After great pain—a formal feeling does come—I—

the society—of that sheer soul. The soul selects
its own society: a formal feeling will come:

I want—Evanescence—slowly. After great pain.
So I refuse to be the only passenger:

I've bought tickets for us to Evanescence, Phil,
and you will be with me as we pass the ghost towns—

What views! Rock ruins of post offices. Brilliant,
Telegraph—we'll pass them. There'll be news from Carthage—

and then Tierra Blanca—the Train holding just us—
Immortality—and Fog—that blond conductor

who will ask—at Chance Village—for our tickets.
You come—punctual as a star!—to wave to the rich,

platforms across us stunned by their luggage. No god
would dare send them away empty, as usual

they're inheriting everything, even hope. See,
there's no end at the end, so you mustn't die, no,

not now, for our train has begun to move, wedding
the sky with a ring of smoke. The rich don't see us,

though we throw roses at them, white and calico,
frail aristocrats of Time. It's far behind now,

mere gold dust, the station of Faraway Nearby,
the rich invisible. And we are millionaires,

passing Pink and Green Mountains, painted just for us,
and other landscapes we own, Black Cross with Red Sky,

Black Mesa, Ghost Ranch Cliffs. Vast Nights of Lightning. Stars.
But your voice is choked, the whisper it was the last

time we spoke. "Let his voice not change!" I'd almost prayed.
You fall silent as I give our tickets to Fog.

When he leaves, we see Light Coming on the Plains,
the last painting we own. As it too vanishes,

you say, "You're wrong. It isn't that my voice has changed.
It's just that you've never before heard it in pain."

10

Shahid, you never
found Evanescence.
And how could

you have? You didn't throw
away addresses from
which streets

departed, erasing
their names. Some
of those streets,

lost at junctions, were
run over by trains.
At stations

where you waited, history
was too late:
those trains

rushed by and disappeared
        into mirrors
                in which

massacres were hushed.
        No reporters
                were allowed

in. You waited to hear
        the glass break,
                but no train

came back. And then
        on those mirrors
                curtains

were drawn. You didn't
        throw away addresses,
                and some

of those streets
        were picked up
                at exits

that took them
        to cities miles
                under the ocean

from where postcards came
           with Africa washed
                   off them.

You didn't throw away
           addresses from which
                   streets

departed. There's
           no one you know
                   in this world.

11

"Phil was afraid of being forgotten."
It's again that summer, Phil, and the end
of that summer again. Good-bye, I am

saying to those students of mist, leaving
Pennsylvania with the sun's reprints.
Ahead is a year of brilliant water —

there's nothing in this world but hope: I have
everyone's address. Everyone will write:
And there's everything in this world but hope.

The Keeper of the Dead Hotel

Still bitterly remembered . . . the
labor strife at the roaring copper
town of Bisbee, leading to the Bisbee
Deportation in July 1917.

In one room upstairs

           he reads late
into the night. Afternoons wake him

to voices speaking in webs. Nights
he lights the desk lamp in the lobby,

then walks into the bar and touches
the piano.

           Drunk senators once gambled
here while their wives blurred

the balconies with silk. One,
an actress whose smile was an era,

came down the steps, turned
like the century to look at herself,

then vanished from the mirror
of the pine hatstand.

           Letters arrived
for her years after. When he reads them,

he hears her whisper: "Something
has happened. What is it?"

No one answers,
but each night a voice cries out: "Fire!"

The copper mountains echo with rifle shots:
men on strike are being killed

in the mines, the survivors forced
into boxcars and left in the desert

without water. Their women are leaving
the city.

       Each night he sees them depart.
Each night he hears laughter from the balconies:

braceleted arms, glasses filled
with the moon's dry wine. Each night

          she still asks:
"Something has happened. What is it?"

But who will tell her? She is furiously
brushing her hair. Her shadow,

through the transom, is soft on the ceiling.
Who will tell her?

       Every silence in the world
has conspired with every other. Unanswered

she is leaving this city again, her voice
pressing him back into the silence

of ash-throated men in the desert,
of broken glasses

on the balconies,
the moon splashed everywhere.

(for John Hudak)

From Another Desert*

Footprints of blood in the path I traveled
lit up the desert, a track of crimson pearls.
—GHALIB

1

Cries Majnoon:

Beloved
you are not here

It is a strange spring
rivers lined with skeletons

Wings beat
in the cages

> letting the wind hear
> its own restlessness
>
> the cry of gods
> and prisoners
>
> letting me hear
> my agony

* The Arabic love story of Qais and Laila is used—in Urdu and Persian literature—to cite the exalting power of love. Qais is called Majnoon (literally "possessed" or "mad") because he sacrificed everything for love. The legend has acquired a political dimension, in that Majnoon can represent the rebel, the revolutionary who is a model of commitment. Laila thus becomes the revolutionary ideal, the goal the Lover/Revolutionary aspires to reach.

2

In the grief of broken stone
among the ghosts of saints and poets
the gods have lost their vermilion marks

No priest comforts their loneliness
in the courtyard of these ruins

only a beggar or two
who lean against the tombs of princes
on which grass

that true cloth
of the beggar

grows wildly—

Look, how a god returns
to his wrecked temple

clings to his marrow
frozen in the bones of his worshipers

touches himself

as he extends the earth
like a begging bowl

in the grief of broken flesh

3

Each statue will be broken
if the heart is a temple. When

the gods return, from the ends
of the fasting sky, they'll stand

in the rain and knock and knock.
They'll force open the heart.

In the grief of ruins, they'll pick
up their severed arms

and depart and depart and depart.

4

There again is memory
at my doorstep —

jasmine crushed under
departing feet.

The moon extinguishes
its silver pain

on the window.

5

Cries Majnoon:

Those in tatters
may now demand love:

　　　I've declared a fashion
　　　of ripped collars.

The breezes are lost
travelers today,

　　　knocking, asking
　　　for a place to stay.

　　　I tell them
　　　to go away.

All night they knock, asking
if the Beloved
had ever passed this way.

> All night I keep
> the heart shut.

I'm waiting
for a greater madness:

> to declare
> myself
> to the Hangman.

6

His blood shines
he is ready to face doom

Just promise him the rain
and pour wine into his glass

His veins illuminated
his blood is ink

He's writing the world's sorrow

His blood is fire

When he arrives in tatters
at the gates of palaces

the beams the arches will burn down

Oh Silence
continue to echo
bring back answers from everywhere

7

Who now weeps
at the crossroads,

remembers the directions
that led so soon

to betrayal,
the disappearance

of all wayfarers
when it was almost

the morning?
Some went back,

folding breezes
in their wallets.

Some ran ahead,
the sun divided

among them, eclipses
hidden in their eyes.

8

Majnoon was again sighted
in the streets, intoxicated

as before, surpassing the rapture
of every mad lover.

9

Majnoon
what will be revealed
by thinking the centuries to glass?

Look at this Persian miniature

In the lush wilderness of sorrow
your father

distempered with a blue innocence
has searched for you
among the living and the dead

Now he rests his head on an uncut sapphire
bereft of prayer

while in margins of gold
verses wear bracelets of paisleys
tied into golden knots of Arabic

and in another miniature
the world goes on
without you:

A royal hunt in a delicate jungle

Horses gallop to the rhythm
of a dying dynasty
the elephants' trunks curled into numerals

On a tree a giant spider
its legs sharpened into pencils
presses their lead into the cobra's crown

The earth is a calligraphy of coils
a carpet of grass woven into scales

and in a cloak laced with prayer
Prince Jehangir

soon to be Emperor of Hindustan
rides the tiger

Ruby buttons glisten on his coat
drops of blood
that have caught him by the collar

Oh Majnoon
there is no justice

He will not dismount
in your wilderness of sorrow

10

In prison Majnoon weeps for Satan:

And Iblis angel of smokeless fire bereft of dreams would still not
bow to man Qais weep for Iblis a lover like you lover of God that
cruel Beloved Qais welcome the knives the stones but never bow to
man learn from Iblis survive somehow survive in Hell each day this
memory the echo of the Beloved's voice telling one to go to Hell

11

The prisoners know they've been
eclipsed, that someone

greater than them is now
among them. For though they know

the rattle of bound ankles,
they've never heard

such sorrow before,
this pounding, this beating down the floor,

this plaint,
all night, of feet in chains.

12

Ambushed in century after century by the police of God
the broken Ishmaels cry out in the blazing noons

welcoming the knives the stones rained down on them

again declared madmen by the government of Sorrow

And Majnoon also among them with bare hands
digs graves in the desert

crying out for his dead Laila

his back broken by a giant teardrop
inside it the ruins of Jerusalem or Beirut

or another rival to the garden of paradise
where his heart broke and broke centuries ago

13

The dead are here. Listen to survivors
search for screams to place on the corpses' mouths.

The self is lost, erased at this moment.
So reveal, quickly, a secret to me:

When, at last, that hour comes, who will lead me
through the catacombs to the swordsman's arms?

Will it be a long-lost friend, speaking of her,
of her hands digging out turquoise perfumes

from the air's mines? Will he bring a message
from her eyes, so far away now, gazing

at a dream in which the ghosts of prisoners
are shaking the bars till iron softens

into a song—everywhere the shadows
of my voice, everywhere a smokeless fire?

Tonight the air is many envelopes
again. Tell her to open them at once

and find hurried notes about my longing
for wings. Tell her to speak, when that hour comes,

simply of the sky. Friend, speak of the sky
when that hour comes. Speak, simply, of the air.

No,

not in the clear stream,
I went fishing in the desert sky.
With rain-hooks at the sun's end,
I caught a rainbow, its colors
slippery in my hands.
I gently separated,
like the bones of a trout,
the blue from the red,
the green from the yellow,
my knife sharp, silver-exact,
each color lean,
impeccably carved.
But the rainbow's end,
though I cleaned and washed
the earth from it,
tasted bitter,
like gold.

Résumé

Below me, always below me is water.
—FRANCIS PONGE

I
an applicant
to the water's green offices
sign my name above a thin horizon

below it reflections
of temples and mosques
a postscript on God

I wait for the sapphire
gossip of stars

but those who promised
to recommend me

place the moon's blank sheets
in my hands unsigned

Who are these authorities
with files of xeroxed rumors?

I hear orders

The clerk of climates
tears up my forms

no opening he says
no vacant reflection

only the rusted wars
and jets dissolving

in a smoke-red twilight

but if I will accept—and I say Yes

Maybe he says Maybe—and I say Yes

above me a quick ceiling of ice
I the secretary of memory
in chambers of weeds

the water's breathless bureaucracy

Notes on the Sea's Existence

1

Yellow island, yellow sun:
My struggle began
with a soft wave,
which offered love
on the shore's terms.
Wearing a mask of glares,
the white, white sand
touched me with fire.

I held myself together,
a still breath.

2

It pulls me to itself,
the reflection, no, not mine:
I know the water's fidelity,

its utter transparence. The sea
becomes me like nothing
else: I wear it like skin.

Who pulls me with such
ease? A dead ancestor,
a lost friend, or

the shell's hollow cry?
The weeds wrap me, like arms.
I'm pulled down, down, to the tip of the sky.

I hold the world as I drown.

Medusa

"I must be beautiful.
Or why would men be speechless
at my sight? I have populated the countryside
with animals of stone
and put nations painlessly to sleep.

I too was human, I who now live here
at the end of the world
with two aging sisters, spinsters
massaging poisons into our scalps
and sunning our ruffled snakes,

and dreading the night, when
under the warm stars
we recall men we have loved,
their gestures now forever refusing us.

Then why let anything remain
when whatever we loved
turned instantly to stone?
I am waiting for the Mediterranean
to see me: It will petrify.
And as caravans from Africa begin to cross it,
I will freeze their cargo of slaves.

Soon, soon, the sky will have eyes:
I will fossilize its dome into cracked blue,
I who am about to come
into God's full view
from the wrong side of the mirror
into which He gazes."

    And so she dreams
    till the sun-crimsoned shield
    blinds her into nightmare:
    her locks, falling from their roots,
    crawl into rocks to die.
    Perseus holds the sword above her neck.
    Restless in her sleep, she,
    for the last time, brushes back
    the hissing curls from her forehead.

The Youngest of the Graeae*

Listen to my account as the world vanishes:
we were young, my sisters and I,
though withered from birth, our hair gray,
in this land of wavering light,
everything shrouded, the sun banished, the moon in exile.

We had the shapes of swans but we had arms,
under our wings of watered silk
our hands ready to take over
the twilight each time one finished
her ration of sight.

It now is mine, this twilight all mine:
my sisters are dead, and I alone am left
to see these trees, these forests, this ebony ocean.

There were times I would have run away
but Sisters, your dreamless faces stopped me,
the blue smoke rising from your sockets.

And what would have been out there in the world?
Only cages and torturing hands,
someone stitching our eye as a trophy
to a screen speckled with mirrors.

* The Graeae, three sisters, shared one eye and lived in a land of perpetual twilight. Gray-haired from birth, they were the sisters and protectors of the Gorgons. Perseus stole their eye and did not return it till they told him how to find the Gorgon Medusa, thus betraying their sister.

Sisters, when I lie
as we did, with my body in the ocean,
my hair thrown like gray waves upon the sand,
I remember what we betrayed
for this twilight.

And I weep on the necks of trees,
praying,

       O God of Light,
before I end this life,
lower your hands into the east
and bring up the sun, once.

Desert Landscape

*Who hath measured the waters
in the hollow of his hand.*
— Isaiah 40:12

Stringing red serrano peppers, crushing
cilantro seeds — just a few yards from where,
in 1693, a Jesuit priest
began to build a boat, bringing rumors
of water to an earth still forgetting

the sea it had lost over two hundred
million years ago — three white-haired women,
their faces young, are guarding the desert
as it gives up its memories of water
(the fossils of vanished species) while miles

from them the sky opens its hands above
a city being brought to memory by rain:
as silver veins erupt over the peaks
and the mountains catch fire, the three women
can see across the veiled miles the streets turn

to streams, then rivers, the poor running from
one another into each other's arms;
can see the moon drown, its dimmed heart gone out
like a hungry child's; can see its corpse rising —
for two have turned toward the dawn, their eyes

holding children washed from their mothers' arms,
and the third, her face against the dark sky
but her fingers slowly white, has let drop
her string of dried peppers and is bringing
the sea — a hollow fossil — to her ear.

I See Chile in My Rearview Mirror

By dark the world is once again intact,
Or so the mirrors, wiped clean, try to reason . . .
—JAMES MERRILL

This dream of water—what does it harbor?
I see Argentina and Paraguay
under a curfew of glass, their colors
breaking, like oil. The night in Uruguay

is black salt. I'm driving toward Utah,
keeping the entire hemisphere in view—
Colombia vermilion, Brazil blue tar,
some countries wiped clean of color: Peru

is titanium white. And always oceans
that hide in mirrors: when beveled edges
arrest tides or this world's destinations
forsake ships. There's Sedona, Nogales

far behind. Once I went through a mirror—
from there too the world, so intact, resembled
only itself. When I returned I tore
the skin off the glass. The sea was unsealed

by dark, and I saw ships sink off the coast
of a wounded republic. Now from a blur
of tanks in Santiago, a white horse
gallops, riderless, chased by drunk soldiers

in a jeep; they're firing into the moon.
And as I keep driving in the desert,
someone is running to catch the last bus, men
hanging on to its sides. And he's missed it.

He is running again; crescents of steel
fall from the sky. And here the rocks
are under fog, the cedars a temple,
Sedona carved by the wind into gods —

each shadow their worshiper. The siren
empties Santiago; he watches
—from a hush of windows—blindfolded men
blurred in gleaming vans. The horse vanishes

into a dream. I'm passing skeletal
figures carved in 700 B.C.
Whoever deciphers these canyon walls
remains forsaken, alone with history,

no harbor for his dream. And what else will
this mirror now reason, filled with water?
I see Peru without rain, Brazil
without forests—and here in Utah a dagger

of sunlight: it's splitting—it's the summer
solstice—the quartz center of a spiral.
Did the Anasazi know the darker
answer also—given now in crystal

by the mirrored continent? The solstice,
but of winter? A beam stabs the window,
diamonds him, a funeral in his eyes.
In the lit stadium of Santiago,

this is the shortest day. He's taken there.
Those about to die are looking at him,
his eyes the ledger of the disappeared.
What will the mirror try now? I'm driving,

still north, always followed by that country,
its floors ice, its citizens so lovesick
that the ground—sheer glass—of every city
is torn up. They demand the republic

give back, jeweled, their every reflection.
They dig till dawn but find only corpses.
He has returned to this dream for his bones.
The waters darken. The continent vanishes.

Snow on the Desert

"Each ray of sunshine is seven minutes old,"
Serge told me in New York one December night.

"So when I look at the sky, I see the past?"
"Yes, yes," he said. "Especially on a clear day."

On January 19, 1987,
as I very early in the morning
drove my sister to Tucson International,

suddenly on Alvernon and 22nd Street
the sliding doors of the fog were opened,

and the snow, which had fallen all night, now
sun-dazzled, blinded us, the earth whitened

out, as if by cocaine, the desert's plants,
its mineral-hard colors extinguished,
wine frozen in the veins of the cactus.

. . .

The Desert Smells Like Rain: in it I read:
The syrup from which sacred wine is made

is extracted from the saguaros each
summer. The Papagos place it in jars,

where the last of it softens, then darkens
into a color of blood though it tastes

strangely sweet, almost white, like a dry wine.
As I tell Sameetah this, we are still

seven miles away. "And you know the flowers
of the saguaros bloom only at night?"

We are driving slowly, the road is glass.
"Imagine where we are was a sea once.

Just imagine!" The sky is relentlessly
sapphire, and the past is happening quickly:

the saguaros have opened themselves, stretched
out their arms to rays millions of years old,

in each ray a secret of the planet's
origin, the rays hurting each cactus

into memory, a human memory—
for they are human, the Papagos say:

not only because they have arms and veins
and secrets. But because they too are a tribe,

vulnerable to massacre. "It is like
the end, perhaps the beginning of the world,"

Sameetah says, staring at their snow-sleeved
arms. And we are driving by the ocean

that evaporated here, by its shores,
the past now happening so quickly that each

stoplight hurts us into memory, the sky
taking rapid notes on us as we turn

at Tucson Boulevard and drive into
the airport, and I realize that the earth

is thawing from longing into longing and
that we are being forgotten by those arms.

. . .

At the airport I stared after her plane
till the window was

                again a mirror.
As I drove back to the foothills, the fog

shut its doors behind me on Alvernon,
and I breathed the dried seas

                the earth had lost,
their forsaken shores. And I remembered

another moment that refers only
to itself:

in New Delhi one night
as Begum Akhtar sang, the lights went out.

It was perhaps during the Bangladesh War,
perhaps there were sirens,

air-raid warnings.
But the audience, hushed, did not stir.

The microphone was dead, but she went on
singing, and her voice

was coming from far
away, as if she had already died.

And just before the lights did flood her
again, melting the frost

of her diamond
into rays, it was, like this turning dark

of fog, a moment when only a lost sea
can be heard, a time

to recollect
every shadow, everything the earth was losing,

a time to think of everything the earth
and I had lost, of all

          that I would lose,
of all that I was losing.

THE COUNTRY WITHOUT
A POST OFFICE

The Blessèd Word: A Prologue

I

From an untitled poem, that opening line announces heartbreak as its craft: a promise like that already holds its own breaking: "We shall meet again, in Petersburg / as though we had buried the sun there."

From Kashmir, that Vale where the Titans sought refuge, where, just before Saturn began to speak to Thea, "There was a listening fear in her regard / As if calamity had but begun," from there: "When you leave home in the morning, you never know if you'll return." "We shall meet again, in Srinagar," I want to answer Irfan. But such a promise? I make it in Mandelstam's velvet dark, in the black velvet Void.

II

Let me cry out in that void, say it as I can. I write on that void: Kashmir, Kaschmir, Cashmere, Qashmir, Cashmir, Cashmire, Kashmere, Cachemire, Cushmeer, Cachmiere, Cašmir. Or *Cauchemar* in a sea of stories? Or: Kacmir, Kaschemir, Kasmere, Kachmire, Kasmir. Kerseymere?

171

He reinvents Petersburg (I, Srinagar), an imaginary homeland, filling it, closing it, shutting himself (myself) in it. For there is the blessèd word with no meaning, there are flowers that will never die, roses that will never fall, a night in which Mandelstam is not afraid and needs no pass. The blessèd women are still singing.

A patrol is stationed on the bridge and a car hoots like a cuckoo.

Maybe the ages will die away and the loved hands of blessèd women will brush the light ashes together?

III

And the night's sun there in Srinagar? Guns shoot stars into the sky, the storm of constellations night after night, the infinite that rages on. It was Id-uz-Zuha: a record of God's inability, for even He must melt sometimes, to let Ishmael be executed by the hand of his father. Srinagar was under curfew. The identity pass may or may not have helped in the crackdown. Son after son—never to return from the night of torture—was taken away.

IV

And will the blessèd women rub the ashes together? Each fall they gather *chinar* leaves, singing what the hills have reechoed for four hundred years, the songs of Habba Khatun, the peasant girl who became the queen. When her husband was exiled from the Valley by the Moghul king Akbar, she went among the people with her sorrow. Her grief, alive to this day, in her own roused the people into frenzied opposition to Moghul rule. And since then Kashmir has never been free.

And will the blesséd women rub the ashes together? Each fall, they sing her songs. They create their rustic fuel for winter: they set fire to the leaves, sprinkle water on them as they burn, and transform them into fragile coals.

But the reports are true, and without song: mass rapes in the villages, towns left in cinders, neighborhoods torched. "Power is hideous / like a barber's hands." The rubble of downtown Srinagar stares at me from the *Times*.

Maybe the ages will die away—we will pray in Mandelstam's night—and the loved hands of blesséd women will brush the light ashes together?

V

And that blesséd word with no meaning—who will utter it? What is it? Will the women pronounce it, as if scripturing the air, for the first time? Or the last?

Srinagar hunches like a wild cat: lonely sentries, wretched in bunkers at the city's bridges, far from their homes in the plains, licensed to kill . . . while the Jhelum flows under them, sometimes with a dismembered body. On Zero Bridge the jeeps rush by. The candles go out as travelers, unable to light up the velvet Void.

What is the blesséd word? Mandelstam gives no clue. One day the Kashmiris will pronounce that word truly for the first time.

(for Irfan Hasan)

Farewell

Solitudinum faciunt et pacem appellant.
    —TACITUS (speaking through a British chieftain regarding Pax Romana)

At a certain point I lost track of you.

They make a desolation and call it peace.

When you left even the stones were buried:

The defenceless would have no weapons.

When the ibex rubs itself against the rocks, who collects
        its fallen fleece from the slopes?

O Weaver whose seams perfectly vanished, who weighs the
        hairs on the jeweler's balance?

They make a desolation and call it peace.

Who is the guardian tonight of the Gates of Paradise?

My memory is again in the way of your history.

Army convoys all night like desert caravans:

In the smoking oil of dimmed headlights, time dissolved—all
        winter—its crushed fennel.

We can't ask them: *Are you done with the world?*

In the lake the arms of temples and mosques are locked
in each other's reflections.

Have you soaked saffron to pour on them when they are
found like this centuries later in this country
I have stitched to your shadow?

in this country we step out with doors in our arms.

Children run out with windows in their arms.

You drag it behind you in lit corridors.

If the switch is pulled you will be torn from everything.

At a certain point I lost track of you.

You needed me. You needed to perfect me:

In your absence you polished me into the Enemy.

Your history gets in the way of my memory.

I am everything you lost. You can't forgive me.

I am everything you lost. Your perfect enemy.

Your memory gets in the way of my memory:

I am being rowed through Paradise on a river of Hell:
    Exquisite ghost, it is night.

The paddle is a heart; it breaks the porcelain waves:

It is still night. The paddle is a lotus:

I am rowed—as it withers—toward the breeze which is soft as
    if it had pity on me.

If only somehow you could have been mine, what wouldn't
    have happened in this world?

I'm everything you lost. You won't forgive me.

My memory keeps getting in the way of your history.

There is nothing to forgive. You won't forgive me.

I hid my pain even from myself; I revealed my pain only to
    myself.

There is everything to forgive. You can't forgive me.

If only somehow you could have been mine,

what would not have been possible in the world?

(for Patricia O'Neill)

I See Kashmir from New Delhi at Midnight

Now and in time to be,
Wherever green is worn, . . .
A terrible beauty is born.
— W. B. YEATS

1

One must wear jeweled ice in dry plains
to will the distant mountains to glass.
The city from where no news can come
is now so visible in its curfewed night
that the worst is precise:

                    From Zero Bridge
a shadow chased by searchlights is running
away to find its body. On the edge
of the Cantonment, where Gupkar Road ends,
it shrinks almost into nothing, is

nothing by Interrogation gates
so it can slip, unseen, into the cells:
Drippings from a suspended burning tire
are falling on the back of a prisoner,
the naked boy screaming, "I know nothing."

2

The shadow slips out, beckons *Console Me*,
and somehow there, across five hundred miles,
I'm sheened in moonlight, in emptied Srinagar,
but without any assurance for him.

On Residency Road, by Mir Pan House,
unheard we speak: "I know those words by heart
(you once said them by chance): In autumn
when the wind blows sheer ice, the *chinar* leaves
fall in clusters—

                  one by one, otherwise."
"Rizwan, it's you, Rizwan, it's you," I cry out
as he steps closer, the sleeves of his *phiren* torn.
"Each night put Kashmir in your dreams," he says,
then touches me, his hands crusted with snow,
whispers, "I have been cold a long, long time."

3

"Don't tell my father I have died," he says,
and I follow him through blood on the road
and hundreds of pairs of shoes the mourners
left behind, as they ran from the funeral,
victims of the firing. From windows we hear
grieving mothers, and snow begins to fall
on us, like ash. Black on edges of flames,
it cannot extinguish the neighborhoods,
the homes set ablaze by midnight soldiers.
Kashmir is burning:

By that dazzling light
we see men removing statues from temples.
We beg them, "Who will protect us if you leave?"
They don't answer, they just disappear
on the road to the plains, clutching the gods.

4

I won't tell your father you have died, Rizwan,
but where has your shadow fallen, like cloth
on the tomb of which saint, or the body
of which unburied boy in the mountains,
bullet-torn, like you, his blood sheer rubies
on Himalayan snow?

                        I've tied a knot
with green thread at Shah Hamdan, to be
untied only when the atrocities
are stunned by your jeweled return, but no news
escapes the curfew, nothing of your shadow,
and I'm back, five hundred miles, taking off
my ice, the mountains granite again as I see
men coming from those Abodes of Snow
with gods asleep like children in their arms.

                    (for Molvi Abdul Hai)

The Last Saffron

Next to saffron cultivation in interest come the floating gardens of the Dal Lake that can be towed from place to place.

1

I will die, in autumn, in Kashmir,
and the shadowed routine of each vein
will almost be news, the blood censored,
for the *Saffron Sun* and the *Times of Rain*

will be sold in black, then destroyed,
invisibly at Zero Taxi Stand.
There will be men nailing tabloids
to the fence of Grindlay's Bank,

I will look for any sign of blood
in captions under the photos of boys,
those who by inches—after the April flood—
were killed in fluted waters, each voice

torn from its throat as the Jhelum
receded to their accounts and found cash
sealed in the bank's reflection.
I will open the waves, draw each hushed

balance, ready to pay, by any means,
whatever the drivers ask. The one
called *Eyes of Maple Green*
will promise, "I'll take you anywhere, even

in curfew hours," and give me a bouquet—
"There's a ban on wreaths!"

2

I will die that day in late October, it will be long ago:

He will take me to Pampore where I'll gather flowers and run
back to the taxi, stamens — How many thousands? — crushed to red
varnish in my hands: I'll shout: "Saffron, my payment!" And he'll
break the limits, chase each rumor of me. "No one's seen Shahid,"
we'll hear again and again, in every tea house from Nishat to Naseem.
He will stop by the Shalimar *ghats*, and we'll descend the steps to
the water. He'll sever some land — two yards — from the shore, I,
his last passenger. Suddenly he'll age, his voice will break, his gaze
green water, washing me: "It won't grow again, this gold from the
burned fields of Pampore." And he will row the freed earth past the
Security zones, so my blood is news in the *Saffron Sun* setting on
the waves.

3

               Yes, I remember it,
the day I'll die, I broadcast the crimson,

so long ago of that sky, its spread air,
its rushing dyes, and a piece of earth

bleeding, apart from the shore, as we went
on the day I'll die, past the guards, and he,

keeper of the world's last saffron, rowed me
on an island the size of a grave. On

two yards he rowed me into the sunset,
past all pain. On everyone's lips was news

of my death but only that beloved couplet,
broken, on his:

"If there is a paradise on earth,
It is this, it is this, it is this."

(for Vidur Wazir)

I Dream I Am the Only Passenger
on Flight 423 to Srinagar,

and when we — as if from ashes — ascend
into the cold where the heart must defend

its wings of terror and even pity
and below us the haze of New Delhi

grays, *In your eyes I look for my wounds' deep sea.*
But five hundred years waved with history?

It is to song that one must turn for flight.
But with what measure will I shed sunlight

on pain? *In your eyes* — Was her sari turquoise? —
I look for the deep sea . . . That is her voice —

Begum Akhtar's. "You were the last, we know,
to see her in Delhi, Desperado

in search of catastrophe." Heartbreak of perfume
is mine again. The pilot turns up the volume:

Attar — of jasmine? What was it she wore
that late morning in October '74

when we were driven (it was the sunniest
day) from Connaught Place to Palam Airport? She pressed

a note — Rs. 100 — into my palm:
"Take it or, on my life, I will perish."

They announced DEPARTURE. I touched her arm.
Her sari *was* turquoise! She turned to vanish,

but then turned to wave. (*My silk is stained,
How will I face my Lord?* she'd set in Pain—

her chosen raga that July in Srinagar.)
A week later: GHAZAL QUEEN BEGUM AKHTAR

IS DEAD. She had claimed her right-to-die:
She had sung "Everyone Will Be Here But I"

those days in every city and trebled that nocturne
desperately—with love—to aubade.

Drunk one night, she had wept, "Shahid, I yearn
to die." What was her encore there in Ahmedabad—

the last song of her last concert? In the middle
of the night they took her to Intensive Care.

Alone, in words whirled in the hospital,
her heart had set—forever solitaire.

The hostess pours tea, hands me the *Statesman*:
31 October 1974?
BEGUM AKHTAR IS DEAD: under the headline:

her picture: she smiles: she lights a Capstan.

Sharp in flame, her face dissolves in smoke.

IT'S WAR:

It's 1994: ARMY LAYS SIEGE TO SHRINE,

and on the intercom her ghazal fades . . .
The pilot's voice brings the news alive. Below us,
the mountains quicken cremation's shades,

and up here the sky rainbows itself. Was it thus
that Lal Ded—robed in the brilliant green
of Paradise—rose from her ashes, fabulous

with *My body blazed?* Could she have then foreseen
the tongue survive its borrowed alphabets?
She blessed her true heir: Sheikh Noor-ud-Din.

He still speaks through five centuries of poets.
I hear his voice: "Fire moves on its quick knees—
through Chrar-e-Sharif—toward my shrine. Know it's

time to return there—before ash filigrees
roses carved in the wood of weeping trees."

I ask, "Will the dry branches, Prophesier,
blaze again with blossom? *On its pyre*

the phoenix is dear to destiny." We begin
our descent. "All threads must be untied

186

before springtime. Ask all—Muslim and Brahmin—
if their wish came true?" He appears beside

me, cloaked in black: "Alas! Death has bent my back.
It is too late for threads at Chrar-e-Sharif."

The landing gear roars, we touch the ashen tarmac.
He holds my hand speechless to tell me if

those smashed golds flying past those petrified
reds are autumn's last crimsoned spillage

rushing with wings down the mountainside
or flames clinging to a torched village.

(for Krishna Misri)

"Some Vision of the World Cashmere"

> *If I could bribe them by a Rose*
> *I'd bring them every flower that grows*
> *From Amherst to Cashmere!*
> — EMILY DICKINSON

I

But the phone rings, here in Amherst: "Your grandmother is dying. Our village is across the bridge over the flood channel, the bridge named for Mahjoor."

"There's no such village!"

"She had a terrible fall. There is curfew everywhere. We have no way to bring her back. There is panic on the roads. Our neighbors have died."

There never was such a village . . .

"We are your relatives from her mother's mother's side. You've heard of us! We once were traders and sold silk carpets to princes in Calcutta, but now we are poor and you have no reason to know us."

II

I put the phone down in Srinagar and run into the sunlight toward her cottage in our garden. Except for her dressing table mirror which Sikander, so long dead, is polishing, the army has occupied her house, made it their dingy office, dust everywhere, on old phones, on damp files, on broken desks. In her drawing room a clerk types. The colonel, dictating, turns around. My lost friend Vir! Srinagar is his city, too, he wouldn't have ordered its burning. It's not him. Someone else with a smile just as kind, the face of a man who in dreams saves nations. Or razes cities.

"My grandmother is ill. Please send someone with me. Please, someone with me in one of your jeeps to the village."

III

In her room the sun shines on her father—a painting from which he stares, unblinded, at even today's sunlight.

Just then through the back gate some villagers and her dead brother are bringing her slowly through the poplars, by the roses. I run out: *Thank God you're alive!* She is telling her brother, *Be grateful you died before these atrocities. My small home a dark office! How will I welcome you?*

IV

The mirrors have grieved in her absence. They run to greet her at the door. It is her home again! Sikander has turned on the radio: a song of Mahjoor's, in Raj Begum's voice: "The whole universe is worth nothing more than your shadow." And I'm holding her hand in that sun which is shining on all the summers of my childhood, shining on a teardrop in which windows are opening, amplifying her voice, and she is telling me, *God is merciful, God is compassionate.*

"Lo, A Tint Cashmere! / Lo, A Rose!"

—EMILY DICKINSON

I

There was another summer: we were listening to Radio Kashmir: the bell announced that second of the sunset: we broke our fasts: then a song:

Now again, summer: a summer of the last Yes: we are in the verandah, listening: on Radio Kashmir, a song: "What can one surrender but the heart? / I yield my remaining years to you."

She is still somehow holding the world together: she is naming the roses:

God loves me, no, He's in love with me, He is a jealous God, He can't bear my love for you, and you are my favorite grandchild. My poet grandson, why don't you write of love?

She is reliving with me her dream within a dream within a dream: the mirrors compete for her reflection: I see her with endless arms: I see her without beginning middle or end: it is the last summer of peace: it is the last summer of the last Yes: we are still somehow holding the world together: we are naming the roses: she lifts her lines of Fate and Life and Heart and Mind and presses them, burning, into my palms. And then Lo, in her empty hands, I see a Rose!

II

"So there is Revolution each day in the heart, / Let Sorrow's resplendent autocracy remain."

Now again, summer: a summer of the last Yes: we are in the verandah, listening:

"So there is Revolution each day in the heart" . . . *That must be Faiz? I stopped praying once. Once. "The earth cried out as I bent my forehead to the ground: / You've crushed me forever with the weight of your faith."*

III

She is still somehow holding the world together: she is naming the roses:

Listen, some winters ago I was with Nasir in Delhi. Word came from America: Nuzhat was dying. And I was left alone. Only his alcoholic servant and I! I fell ill, I couldn't walk. The servant said: This is God's will! A nurse from the nearby dispensary gave me an injection. I fell into some half-dream, half-sleep, in fever—I don't know how long. I see three women, two I recognized, but who is the third? I must be dead and they've come to bury me. No, they will persuade me to live! In a nursing home, they gave me a beautiful room. Outside my window the garden is full of flowers. And I am dead and this is Paradise and what a beautiful place God has given me.

IV

Her dream within a dream within a dream:

Then through the window I see my father and my husband. They were so young. They are coming toward me, and I wake up in the dream and tell the doctor, Don't prolong my agony, don't you see, my husband and father have come to call me. The doctor is telling those women, She's not cooperating. No, I will take the medicines, I don't want to die. But I see my husband and my father—O how long they have been dead! They are so young! They are in the garden and I am dead and I must have done good for God to grant me this world of flowers.

Ghazal

Pale hands I loved beside the Shalimar
—LAURENCE HOPE

Where are you now? Who lies beneath your spell tonight
before you agonize him in farewell tonight?

Pale hands that once loved me beside the Shalimar:
Whom else from rapture's road will you expel tonight?

Those "Fabrics of Cashmere—" "to make Me beautiful—"
"Trinket"—to gem—"Me to adorn—How—tell"—tonight?

I beg for haven: Prisons, let open your gates—
A refugee from Belief seeks a cell tonight.

Executioners near the woman at the window.
Damn you, Elijah, I'll bless Jezebel tonight.

Lord, cried out the idols, *Don't let us be broken*;
Only we can convert the infidel tonight.

Has God's vintage loneliness turned to vinegar?
He's poured rust into the Sacred Well tonight.

In the heart's veined temple all statues have been smashed.
No priest in saffron's left to toll its knell tonight.

He's freed some fire from ice, in pity for Heaven;
he's left open—for God—the doors of Hell tonight.

And I, Shahid, only am escaped to tell thee—
God sobs in my arms. Call me Ishmael tonight.

Dear Shahid,

*No idea, even an idea as close to many Russians as the indivisibility of Russia, can
justify a war against a whole people.*
—ELENA BONNER, open letter to Yeltsin on Chechnya

No human being or group of people has the right to pass a death sentence on a city.
—CHARLES SIMIC

I am writing to you from your far-off country. Far even from us
who live here. Where you no longer are. Everyone carries his address
in his pocket so that at least his body will reach home.

Rumors break on their way to us in the city. But word still reaches
us from border towns: Men are forced to stand barefoot in snow
waters all night. The women are alone inside. Soldiers smash radios
and televisions. With bare hands they tear our houses to pieces.

You must have heard Rizwan was killed. Rizwan: Guardian of
the Gates of Paradise. Only eighteen years old. Yesterday at Hideout
Café (everyone there asks about you), a doctor—who had just treated
a sixteen-year-old boy released from an interrogation center—said: I
*want to ask the fortune-tellers: Did anything in his line of Fate reveal that the
webs of his hands would be cut with a knife?*

This letter, *insh'Allah*, will reach you for my brother goes south
tomorrow where he shall post it. Here one can't even manage postage
stamps. Today I went to the post office. Across the river. Bags and
bags—hundreds of canvas bags—all undelivered mail. By chance I
looked down and there on the floor I saw this letter addressed to you.
So I am enclosing it. I hope it's from someone you are longing for
news of.

Things here are as usual though we always talk about you. Will you come soon? Waiting for you is like waiting for spring. We are waiting for the almond blossoms. And, if God wills, O! those days of peace when we all were in love and the rain was in our hands wherever we went.

A Pastoral

on the wall the dense ivy of executions
—ZBIGNIEW HERBERT

We shall meet again, in Srinagar,
by the gates of the Villa of Peace,
our hands blossoming into fists
till the soldiers return the keys
and disappear. Again we'll enter
our last world, the first that vanished

in our absence from the broken city.
We'll tear our shirts for tourniquets
and bind the open thorns, warm the ivy
into roses. Quick, by the pomegranate—
the bird will say—Humankind can bear
everything. No need to stop the ear

to stories rumored in branches: We'll hear
our gardener's voice, the way we did
as children, clear under trees he'd planted:
"It's true, my death, at the mosque entrance,
in the massacre, when the Call to Prayer
opened the floodgates"—Quick, follow the silence—

"and dawn rushed into everyone's eyes."
Will we follow the horned lark, pry
open the back gate into the poplar groves,
go past the search post into the cemetery,
the dust still uneasy on hurried graves
with no names, like all new ones in the city?

"It's true" (we'll hear our gardener
again). "That bird is silent all winter.
Its voice returns in spring, a plaintive cry.
That's when it saw the mountain falcon
rip open, in mid-air, the blue magpie,
then carry it, limp from the talons."

Pluck the blood: My words will echo thus
at sunset, by the ivy, but to what purpose?
In the drawer of the cedar stand,
white in the verandah, we'll find letters:
When the post offices died, the mailman
knew we'd return to answer them. Better

if he'd let them speed to death,
blacked out by Autumn's Press Trust—
not like this, taking away our breath,
holding it with love's anonymous
scripts: "See how your world has cracked.
Why aren't you here? Where are you? Come back.

Is history deaf there, across the oceans?"
Quick, the bird will say. And we'll try
the keys, with the first one open the door
into the drawing room. Mirror after mirror,
textiled by dust, will blind us to our return
as we light oil lamps. The glass map of our country,

still on the wall, will tear us to lace —
We'll go past our ancestors, up the staircase,
holding their wills against our hearts. Their wish
was we return — forever! — and inherit (Quick, the bird
will say) that to which we belong, not like this —
to get news of our death after the world's.

(for Suvir Kaul)

Return to Harmony 3

Two summers? Epochs, then, of ice.

But the air is the same muslin, beaten by the sky on Nanga Parbat, then pressed on the rocks of the nearer peaks.

I run down the ramp.

On the tarmac, I eavesdrop on Operation Tiger: Troops will burn down the garden and let the haven remain.

This is home—the haven a cage surrounded by ash—the fate of Paradise.

Through streets strewn with broken bricks and interrupted by paramilitaries, Irfan drives me straight to the Harmonies ("3" for my father—the youngest brother!), three houses built in a pastoral, that walled acreage of Harmonies where no one but my mother was poor.

A bunker has put the house under a spell. Shadowed eyes watch me open the gate, like a trespasser.

Has the gardener fled?

The Annexe of the Harmonies is locked—my grandmother's cottage—where her sons offered themselves to her as bouquets of mirrors. There was nothing else to reflect.

Under the windows the roses have choked in their beds. Was the gardener killed?

And the postman?

In the drawer of the cedar stand peeling in the verandah, a pile of damp letters—one to my father to attend a meeting the previous autumn, another an invitation to a wedding.

My first key opens the door. I break into quiet. The lights work.

The Koran still protects the house, lying strangely wrapped in a *jamawar* shawl where my mother had left it on the walnut table by the fireplace. Above, *If God is with you, Victory is near!*—the framed calligraphy ruthless behind cobwebs.

I pick up the dead phone, its number exiled from its instrument, a refugee among forlorn numbers in some angry office on Exchange Road.

But the receiver has caught a transmission: Rafi's song from a film about war: *Slowly, I so slowly, kept on walking, / and then was severed forever from her.* THIS IS ALL INDIA RADIO, AMRITSAR. I hang up.

Upstairs, the window, too, is a mirror; if I jump through it I will fall into my arms.

The mountains return my stare, untouched by blood.

On my shelf, by Ritsos and Rilke and Cavafy and Lorca and Iqbal and Amichai and Paz, my parents are beautiful in their wedding brocades, so startlingly young!

And there in black and white my mother, eighteen years old, a year before she came a bride to these Harmonies, so unforgivenly poor and so unforgivingly beautiful that the house begins to shake in my arms, and when the unarmed world is still again, with pity, it is the house that is holding me in its arms and the cry coming faded from its empty rooms is my cry.

The Country Without a Post Office

... letters sent
To dearest him that lives alas! away.
—GERARD MANLEY HOPKINS

1

Again I've returned to this country
where a minaret has been entombed.
Someone soaks the wicks of clay lamps
in mustard oil, each night climbs its steps
to read messages scratched on planets.
His fingerprints cancel blank stamps
in that archive for letters with doomed
addresses, each house buried or empty.

Empty? Because so many fled, ran away,
and became refugees there, in the plains,
where they must now will a final dewfall
to turn the mountains to glass. They'll see
us through them—see us frantically bury
houses to save them from fire that, like a wall,
caves in. The soldiers light it, hone the flames,
burn our world to sudden papier-mâché

inlaid with gold, then ash. When the muezzin
died, the city was robbed of every Call.
The houses were swept about like leaves
for burning. Now every night we bury
our houses—and theirs, the ones left empty.

We are faithful. On their doors we hang wreaths.
More faithful each night fire again is a wall
and we look for the dark as it caves in.

2

"We're inside the fire, looking for the dark,"
one card lying on the street says. "I want
to be he who pours blood. To soak your hands.
Or I'll leave mine in the cold till the rain
is ink, and my fingers, at the edge of pain,
are seals all night to cancel the stamps."
The mad guide! The lost speak like this. They haunt
a country when it is ash. Phantom heart,

pray he's alive. I have returned in rain
to find him, to learn why he never wrote.
I've brought cash, a currency of paisleys
to buy the new stamps, rare already, blank,
no nation named on them. Without a lamp
I look for him in houses buried, empty —
He may be alive, opening doors of smoke,
breathing in the dark his ash-refrain:

"Everything is finished, nothing remains."
I must force silence to be a mirror
to see his voice again for directions.
Fire runs in waves. Should I cross that river?
Each post office is boarded up. Who will deliver
parchment cut in paisleys, my news to prisons?
Only silence can now trace my letters
to him. Or in a dead office the dark panes.

3

"The entire map of the lost will be candled.
I'm keeper of the minaret since the muezzin died.
Come soon, I'm alive. There's almost a paisley
against the light, sometimes white, then black.
The glutinous wash is wet on its back
as it blossoms into autumn's final country —
Buy it, I issue it only once, at night.
Come before I'm killed, my voice canceled."

In this dark rain, be faithful, Phantom heart,
this is your pain. Feel it. You must feel it.
"Nothing will remain, everything's finished,"
I see his voice again: "This is a shrine
of words. You'll find your letters to me. And mine
to you. Come soon and tear open these vanished
envelopes." And I reach the minaret:
I'm inside the fire. I have found the dark.

This is your pain. You must feel it. Feel it,
Heart, be faithful to his mad refrain—
For he soaked the wicks of clay lamps,
lit them each night as he climbed these steps
to read messages scratched on planets.
His hands were seals to cancel the stamps.
This is an archive. I've found the remains
of his voice, that map of longings with no limit.

4

I read them, letters of lovers, the mad ones,
and mine to him from whom no answers came.
I light lamps, send my answers, Calls to Prayer
to deaf worlds across continents. And my lament
is cries countless, cries like dead letters sent
to this world whose end was near, always near.
My words go out in huge packages of rain,
go there, to addresses, across the oceans.

It's raining as I write this. I have no prayer.
It's just a shout, held in, it's Us! It's Us!
whose letters are cries that break like bodies
in prisons. Now each night in the minaret
I guide myself up the steps. Mad silhouette,
I throw paisleys to clouds. The lost are like this:
They bribe the air for dawn, this their dark purpose.
But there's no sun here. There is no sun here.

Then be pitiless you whom I could not save—
Send your cries to me, if only in this way:
I've found a prisoner's letters to a lover—
One begins: "These words may never reach you."
Another ends: "The skin dissolves in dew
without your touch." And I want to answer:
I want to live forever. What else can I say?
It rains as I write this. Mad heart, be brave.

(for James Merrill)

The Floating Post Office

*The post boat was like a gondola
that called at each houseboat. It
carried a clerk, weighing scales,
and a bell to announce arrivals.*

Has he been kept from us? Portents
of rain, rumors, ambushed letters . . .
Curtained palanquin, fetch our word,
bring us word: Who has died? Who'll live?
Has the order gone out to close
the waterways . . . the one open road?

And then we saw the boat being rowed
through the fog of death, the sentence
passed on our city. It came close
to reveal smudged black-ink letters
which the postman — he *was* alive —
gave us, like signs, without a word,

and we took them, without a word.
From our deck we'd seen the hill road
bringing a jade rain, near-olive,
down from the temple, some penitent's
cymbaled prayer? He took our letters,
and held them, like a lover, close

to his heart. And the rain drew close.
Was there, we asked, a new password —
blood, blood shaken into letters,
cruel primitive script that would erode
our saffron link to the past? Tense
with autumn, the leaves, drenched olive,

fell on graveyards, crying "O live!"
What future would the rain disclose?
O Rain, abandon all pretense,
now drown the world, give us your word,
ring, sweet assassin of the road,
the temple bell! For if letters

come, I will answer those letters
and my year will be tense, alive
with love! The temple receives the road:
there, the rain has come to a close.
Here the waters rise; our each word
in the fog awaits a sentence:

His hand on the scales, he gives his word:
Our letters will be rowed through olive
canals, tense waters no one can close.

The Correspondent

I say "There's no way back to your country,"
I tell him he must never leave. He cites
the world: his schedule. I set up barricades:
the mountain routes are damp;
there, dead dervishes damascene
the dark. "I must leave now," his voice ablaze.
I take off—it's my last resort—my shadow.

And he walks—there's no electricity—
back into my dark, murmurs *Kashmir!*, lights
(to a soundtrack of exploding grenades)
a dim kerosene lamp.
"We must give back the hour its sheen,
or this spell will never end. . . . Quick," he says,
"I've just come—with videos—from Sarajevo."

His footage is priceless with sympathy,
close-ups in slow motion: from bombed sites
to the dissolve of mosques in colonnades.
Then, wheelchairs on a ramp,
burning. He fast-forwards: the scene:
the sun: a man in formal wear: he plays
on the sidewalk his unaccompanied cello,

the hour tuned, dusk-slowed, to Albinoni,
only the *Adagio* as funeral rites
before the stars dazzle, polished to blades
above a barbed-wire camp.
The cellist disappears. The screen

fills—first with soldiers, then the dead, their gaze
fractured white with subtitles. Whose echo

inhabits the night? The phone rings. I think he
will leave. I ask: "When will the satellites
transmit my songs, carry Kashmir, aubades
always for dawns to stamp
True! across seas?" The stars careen
down, the lamp dies. He hangs up. A haze
settles over us. He opens the window,

points to convoys in the mountains, army
trucks with dimmed lights. He wants exclusive rights
to this dream, its fused quartz of furtive shades.
He's been told to revamp
his stories, reincarnadine
their gloss. I light a candle. He'll erase
Bosnia, I feel. He will rewind to zero,

film from there a way back to his country,
bypassing graves that in blacks and whites
climb ever up the hills. The wax cascades
down the stand, silver clamp
to fasten this dream, end it unseen.
In the faltering light, he surveys
what's left. He zooms madly into my shadow.

A Fate's Brief Memoir

1

A Fate—ask the stars!—gives no interviews,
but Visitor, dark from that doomed planet,
you have climbed the pitiful thread—blue noose

by which your life hangs—so I will let
myself answer you. My sisters should shortly
be here . . . this will be a brief tête-à-tête.

What is [clever question!] *the Fates' destiny?*
Always these scissors, only these scissors,
and in the stars' light each of us lonely

with threads—trillions: Cleopatra's. Caesar's.
O pardon me thou bleeding piece of earth—
I am well-read, you see, not always daggers

drawn. But we know nothing of our own birth.
Suddenly we were here—call us orphans—
beautiful certainly, with ties not worth

our while, each strand recalled by oblivion.
What a scribble, these questions on your sheet:
Do you also spin the threads of nations?

2

Are you feminists? YOU must be an athlete
to have climbed so neatly all this way to us.
We too outwit Ways we cannot defeat —

through dashes — so imagine! To become conscious
thus in this island universe — no past —
born cold holding steel in our hands? Jesus!

I never swear, but . . . notice the thinness
of breaths about to break. We recycle
them wholly black till their cobwebs incandesce

into — see those sheets: our letterheads: no last
name, just: FATE FATE FATE and then for address
(cross it out!) ~~ETERNITY~~. *That* we've outclassed.

3

So cruel then that each star be our jewel
and no one to witness it. For ornament,
my sisters empty nebulas by the fistful —

soon they will be here. The skies are rent
by stillborn suns. So glad that we have met,
that you have come; for, yes, we do miss men . . .

O that way madness lies . . . sweet heaven, O let
me not be mad . . . for when, by reflex, we execute
Heaven's texts—hammered on the Guarded Tablet—

we again learn our weakness: we can't commute
a sentence. My sister's hands—the youngest one's—
shook when she let a nation go. She uproots

stars, plucks them wildly—Call it adolescence—
and with their edges scratches the sky's glass.
After such knowledge what forgiveness? What defence?

At once aristocrat and working class,
keeping threads from entangling was her rapture.
Why should I tell you this? You will leave, alas!

O Fool! I shall go mad. Trespasser,
I must speak a little more. Avatars—
but of what?—we didn't know this would entrap her,

our sister's fingerprints dense on the stars.
Our hands gnarled with cutting, were we so wrong,
institutionalized thus in coeternal hours?

Finally no one is ours. You then will belong
to no one, too—not even me, your executioner.
You of course have known this all along?

I hold your breath. Look, I slow my fingers.
Do you now see why we give no interviews?
When you leave my hands will again be spiders.

What is this underlined? I hate *VALUES* . . .
I only prize a crisp prose: it sharpens
the dullest life. O, I've gone on. Well, spread this news:

PAST PRESENT FUTURE: not for us those prisons —
like the *Norns!* What a name! One thing we know:
we won't be compared with our Icelandic cousins;

they have no manner. Our ties are zero,
thinned with melting dew. We collapse all time —
the privilege of those with time; we go

on. Shall I give myself up (paradigm
from your world) for adoption? Who would refuse
me? *We will greet the time.* I ramble . . . I'm . . .

In this asylum one sings the madder blues.
But stay. Take care. Your hour will soon elapse.
My sisters — see them there — the stars bruise

their hands — rhinestones, really — well, let the chips
fall in whatever black hole. Galactic cluster,
what starry rubbish! Suddenly it's cold. What creeps

in spinning at this petty pace? A stiller
mankind breathes in caves, awaiting the Apocalypse.
No word yet looms of the Executioner.

What news may I give you of that Eclipse?
An implant already beats where the sun
has failed. Some hints then from my chilled lips:

4

There between planets the cobwebs thicken.
Depart now. Spiders look for my heart lest
I forget the final wreck of all that's human.

Farewell—and if thou livest or diest!
What poverty lets death exert its affluence?
The earth will receive you, poor honored guest,

and I minding my threadbare subsistence —
poor host who could offer you nothing. What brocades
spun from gasps I tear to polish our instruments . . .

threads searchlit, the universe dazzled, burnished blades . . .
Feel a new sun pounding — Dear Heart, this once!
See the famished sighs I'll lock into braids.

Don't forget this sight when by desolate chance
from your breath Belovéd! this evening fades.

(for William Wadsworth)

At the Museum

But in 2500 B.C. Harappa,
who cast in bronze a servant girl?

No one keeps records
of soldiers and slaves.

The sculptor knew this,
polishing the ache

off her fingers stiff
from washing the walls

and scrubbing the floors,
from stirring the meat

and the crushed asafoetida
in the bitter gourd.

But I'm grateful she smiled
at the sculptor,

as she smiles at me
in bronze,

a child who had to play woman
to her lord

when the warm June rains
came to Harappa.

A History of Paisley

*Their footsteps formed the paisley when Parvati, angry after a
quarrel, ran away from Shiva. He eventually caught up with her.
To commemorate their reunion, he carved the Jhelum River, as it
moves through the Vale of Kashmir, in the shape of paisley.*

You who will find the dark fossils of paisleys
one afternoon on the peaks of Zabarvan —
Trader from an ancient market of the future,
alibi of chronology, that vain
collaborator of time — won't know that these

are her footprints from the day the world began
when land rushed, from the ocean, toward Kashmir.
And above the rising Himalayas? The air
chainstitched itself till the sky hung its bluest
tapestry. But already — as she ran

away — refugee from her Lord — the ruins
of the sea froze, in glaciers, cast in amber.
And there, in the valley below, the river
beguiled its banks into petrified longing:
(O see, it is still the day the world begins:

and the city rises, holding its remains,
its wooden beams already their own fire's prophets.)
And you, now touching sky, deaf to her anklets
still echoing in the valley, deaf to men
fleeing from soldiers into dead-end lanes

(Look! Their feet bleed; they leave footprints on the street
which will give up its fabric, at dusk, a carpet) —
you have found — you'll think — the first teardrop, gem
that was enticed for a Moghul diadem
into design. For you, blind to all defeat

218

up there in pure sunlight, your gauze of cloud thrown
off your shoulders over the Vale, do not hear
bullets drowning out the bells of her anklets.
This is her relic, but for you the first tear,
drop that you hold as you descend past flowstone,

past dried springs, on the first day of the world.
The street is rolled up, ready for southern ports.
Your ships wait there. What other cargo is yours?
What cables have you sent to tomorrow's bazaars?
What does that past await: the future unfurled

like flags? news from the last day of the world?
You descend quickly, to a garden-café:
At a table by a bed of tzigane
roses, three men are discussing, between
sips of tea, undiscovered routes on emerald

seas, ships with almonds, with shawls bound for Egypt.
It is dusk. The gauze is torn. A weaver kneels,
gathers falling threads. Soon he will stitch the air.
But what has made you turn? Do you hear her bells?
O, alibi of chronology, in what script

in your ledger will this narrative be lost?
In that café, where they discuss the promise
of the world, her cry returns from its abyss
where it hides, by the river. They don't hear it.
The city burns; the dusk has darkened to rust

by the roses. They don't see it. O Trader,
what news will you bring to your ancient market?
I saw her. A city was razed. In its debris
her bells echoed. I turned. They didn't see me
turn to see her—on the peaks—in rapid flight forever.

(for Anuradha Dingwaney)

A Footnote to History

Gypsies:... coming originally from India to Europe a thousand years ago ...

On the banks of the Indus,
just before

       it reaches
       the ocean,

and just before
the monsoons,

       they left
       me clutching

islands of farewells.

For ten centuries
they sent no word

though I often heard
through seashells

ships whispering for help.

I stuffed my pockets
with the sounds of wrecks.

I still can't decipher
scripts of storms

as I leaf through
the river's waves.

Half-torn by the wind,
their words reach

the shore, demanding
I memorize their

ancient and recent
journeys in

caravans ambushed by
forests on fire.

(for Bari Károly)

Son et Lumière at Shalimar Garden

Brahma's voice is torn water:

It runs down

    the slopes of Zabarvan
    and Kashmir is a lake

till a mountain to its west
is pierced with a trident

and the valley drained to reveal
the One Born of Water,

    now easily slain.

Who was that demon
of desiccated water?

No one knows
in the drying land

where a rattle of cones
is thatching

the roofs of kingdoms.

    We watch the wind.
    And unhealed,

the centuries pass:

Slaves plane the mountains
with roots they carried

in trunks from Isfahan:

Spotlights lash their backs
as Shalimar blooms into

the Moghuls' thirst for
terracing the seasons

       into symmetry.
        In the marble summer palace,

a nautch-girl pours wine
into the Emperor's glass,

splintering the future
into wars of succession,

the leaves scattered
as the wind blows

       an era into

another dynasty's bloody arms.

Ghazal

The only language of loss left in the world is Arabic—
These words were said to me in a language not Arabic.

Ancestors, you've left me a plot in the family graveyard—
Why must I look, in your eyes, for prayers in Arabic?

Majnoon, his clothes ripped, still weeps for Laila.
O, this is the madness of the desert, his crazy Arabic.

Who listens to Ishmael? Even now he cries out:
Abraham, throw away your knives, recite a psalm in Arabic.

From exile Mahmoud Darwish writes to the world:
You'll all pass between the fleeting words of Arabic.

The sky is stunned, it's become a ceiling of stone.
I tell you it must weep. So kneel, pray for rain in Arabic.

At an exhibition of miniatures, such delicate calligraphy:
Kashmiri paisleys tied into the golden hair of Arabic!

The Koran prophesied a fire of men and stones.
Well, it's all now come true, as it was said in the Arabic.

When Lorca died, they left the balconies open and saw:
his *qasidas* braided, on the horizon, into knots of Arabic.

Memory is no longer confused, it has a homeland—
Says Shammas: Territorialize each confusion in a graceful Arabic.

Where there were homes in Deir Yassein, you'll see dense forests—
That village was razed. There's no sign of Arabic.

I too, O Amichai, saw the dresses of beautiful women.
And everything else, just like you, in Death, Hebrew, and Arabic.

They ask me to tell them what *Shahid* means—
Listen: It means "The Belovéd" in Persian, "witness" in Arabic.

First Day of Spring

KENT. Is this the promis'd end?
EDGAR. Or image of that horror?
   — King Lear, 5.3.264–65

On this perfect day, perfect for forgetting God,
why are they—Hindu or Muslim, Gentile or Jew—
shouting again some godforsaken word of God?

The Angel, his wings flailing—no, burning—stood awed.
The Belovéd, dark with excessive bright, withdrew
and the day was not perfect for forgetting God.

On a face of stone it bends, the divining rod:
Not silver veins but tears: Niobe, whereunto
your slain children swaddled dark with the Names of God?

And now on earth, you and I, with longing so flawed
that: Angel forced to grow not wings but arms, why aren't you
holding me this day—perfect for forgetting God?

You spent these years on every street in Hell? How odd,
then, that I never saw you there, I who've loved you
against (*Hold me!*) against every word of God.

The rumor? It's again the reign of Nimrod.
Whoever you are, I depend on your message,

                                  but you—

        Angel I suspect no longer of God—
are still bringing me word from (*Could it be?*) from God.

Ghazal

adapted from Makhdoom Mohiuddin

Rumors of spring—they last from dawn till dusk—
All eyes decipher branches for blossoms.

Your legend now equals our thirst, Belovéd—
Your word has spread across broken nations.

Wherever each night I'm lost to myself,
they hear from me of Her—of Her alone.

Hope extinguished, now nothing else remains—
only nights of anguish, these ochre dawns.

The garden's eyes well up, the flower's heart beats
when we speak, just speak of O! Forever.

So it has, and forever it should last—
this rumor the Belovéd shares our pain.

Death Row

Someone else in this world has been mentioning you,

        gathering news, itemizing your lives
for a file you'll never see. He already knows

in which incarnation you won't find what you will
again lose in this one.

        He has traced your every
death. You need him now, but he's still asking about

you, with each question destroying your any chance
to find him. It was he

        whom you lost on your last
night alive in another life: he entered

your cell and you were reborn for that night as
anything he wanted: a woman when

        he asked for the love of women.

(for Hala Moddelmog)

The City of Daughters

God gave Noah the rainbow sign,
No more water; the fire next time!

(1990)

Who has flown in, pitiless, from the plains
with a crystal goblet in which—rum-dark!—
he sees the world? He drinks. And cold, the rains
come down. Now who will save Noah? The Ark

is set aflame, launched. And God? Here,
again, why I believe in Him: He put
his lips to my ear and said Nothing. Share,
then, my heart—anyone! Say farewell, cut

my heart loose, row its boat without me—
for I am leaving my world forever.
Say farewell, say farewell to the city
(O Sarajevo! O Srinagar!),

the Alexandria that is forever leaving.
I'm running toward a barbed-wire fence
and someone is running after me, shouting,
Take your name away, leave us in suspense:

whether you vanished? or survived? Garlands
replace the twisted wires, and I break free . . .
bullets fall, roses!, off me, and in my hands,
without a thread of blood, thorns bury

(1991)

their secrets. *No, Dream, remain with the waters.*
Troops pour into the City of Daughters
(his goblet is taken off the mantel shelf),
and I must row the heart all by myself,

I must row the heart (the world is rum-dark!),
I'll row it, but not by the rainbow's arc . . .
He sees the world; I'll row it by stardust,
I will sink it to find you, if I must,

for in this world below zero Fahrenheit
it's over, the Festival of Light:
From the shore through her hair blown black
a mother sees a fleet depart to sack

a city (a drum mimes the sunset wind:
In *Iphigenia* it's night and THE END . . .
Will you watch as her blood soaks the altar?
O too-late wind that did not save a daughter!) . . .

In the mosques of the city that is leaving
forever — suspended in lamps, with floating
wicks of oil — vessels flare, go out. The years
have come (Promise me, love, you will be there?),

(1993)

when I must spend my time on every street
in Hell. The Governor in his mansion rings
the crystal. It is refilled. The songs
in Sacredhair go out. An imperial fleet

of trucks —*No more water!*—enters the Square.
The shops are set afire. *Where are you, my love,*
in this world dyed orange —in one stroke mauve?
("God's secret: He put His lips to my ear

and didn't say a thing." —Jaime Sabines).
"Dear Shahid, they burned the Palladium."
There, the kiss each weekend at 7:00 P.M.
was enshrined, and we tried it, merciless

to ourselves—we pulled the kiss off the screen.
Then the Angel forced us to shut our eyes
when his wings red-darkened those epic skies:
In *A Tale of Two Cities* the guillotine

did not stop falling . . . *It is a far, far*
better thing that I do . . . But when the martyr
went ("Why wasn't he afraid to die?" cried Caesar),
smiling with each step to death, his lips ajar—

(1994)

targets for a kiss! —our eyes were open.
Now when bullets vine-scatter their petals
on our wall, what's left but the horizon
and a flame's bruised sulfur? After INTERVAL,*

before walls burgeoned petal by petal,
a cigarette was alive in a finished world.
I again smell it, the struck matchstick. It's INTERVAL:
in a mansion rum-dark waters are swirled.

A cigarette was alive, and it's a finished world —
in autumn we planted its final embers.
The Ark rocked. The waters were swirled.
Troops poured into the City of Daughters.

No more water! —We again plant embers.
What's left to abolish in Lal Chowk?
Troops burn down the City of Daughters,
and a tree bursts into branches of smoke.

In his waters it's the end. In Lal Chowk,
what's left to abolish? There is no horizon.
From the tree we are tearing flowers of smoke,
no longer targets for a kiss, but our lips open.

* In South Asia, Interval is the term commonly used for Intermission.

Muharram in Srinagar,* 1992

Death flies in, thin bureaucrat, from the plains—
a one-way passenger, again. The monsoon rains
smash their bangles, like widows, against the mountains.
Our hands disappear. He travels first-class, sipping champagne.

One-way passengers again, the monsoon rains
break their hands. Will ours return, ever, to hold a bouquet?
He travels first-class. Our hands disappear. Sipping champagne,
he goes through the morning schedule for Doomsday:

"Break their hands." Will ours return with guns, or a bouquet?
Ice hardens its fat near his heart. We're cut to the brains.
He memorizes, clause by clause, the contract for Doomsday.
We mourn the martyrs of Karbala, our skins torn with chains.

Ice hardens its fat in his heart, and we're cut to the brains.
Near the ramp colonels wait with garlands by a jeep.
(O mourners, Husain bleeds, tear your skins with chains!)
The plane lands. In the Vale the children are dead, or asleep.

He descends. The colonels salute. A captain starts the jeep.
The Mansion by the lake awaits him with roses. He's driven
through streets bereft of children: they are dead, not asleep.
O, when will our hands return, if only broken?

* Muharram, the Muslim month of mourning, marks the martyrdom of Husain (Prophet
Mohammed's grandson) and his followers in the battle of Karbala.

The Mansion is white, lit up with roses. He is driven
through streets in which blood flows like Husain's.
Our hands won't return to us, not even mutilated, when
Death comes — thin bureaucrat — from the plains.

Hans Christian Ostro

*Even today there are no trains
into the Vale of Kashmir.*

And those defunct trains — Kashmir Mail,
Srinagar Express — took
pilgrims only till the last of the plains.
There, in blue-struck buses, they forsook
the monsoon. What iron could be forged to rail
like faith through mountains

star-sapphired, by dawn amethyst?
It's not a happy sound . . .
There is such pathos in the cry of trains:
Words breathed aloud but inward-bound.
Bruised by trust   O Heart bare amidst
fire   arms turquoise with veins

from love's smoke-mines   blesséd infidel
who wants your surrender?
I cannot protect you: these are my hands.
I'll wait by the deep-jade river;
You'll emerge from the mist of Jewel Tunnel:
O the peaks one commands —

A miracle! — from there . . . Will morning
suffice to dazzle blind
beggars to sight? *Whoso gives life to a soul*
shall be as if he had to all of mankind
given life. Or will your veins' hurt lightning —
the day streaked with charcoal —

betray you, beautiful stranger
sent to a lovelorn people
longing for God? Their river torn apart,
they've tied waves around their ankles,
mourning the train that save its passenger
will at night depart

for drowning towns. And draped in rain
of the last monsoon-storm,
a beggar, ears pressed to that metal cry,
will keep waiting on a ghost-platform,
holding back his tears, waving every train
Good-bye and Good-bye.*

* Hans Christian Ostro was a twenty-seven-year-old Norwegian hostage
killed in Kashmir by the Al-Faran militants in August 1995.

A Villanelle

When the ruins dissolve like salt in water,
only then will they have destroyed everything.
Let your blood till then embellish the slaughter,

till dawn soaks up its inks, and "On their blotter
of fog the trees / Seem a botanical drawing."
Will the ruins dissolve like salt in water?

A woman combs—at noon—the ruins for her daughter.
Chechnya is gone. What roses will you bring—
plucked from shawls at dusk—to wreathe the slaughter?

Or are these words plucked from God that you've brought her,
this comfort: *They will not have destroyed everything*
till the ruins, too, are destroyed? Like salt in water,

what else besides God disappears at the altar?
O Kashmir, Armenia once vanished. Words are nothing,
just rumors—like roses—to embellish a slaughter:

these of a columnist: "The world will not stir";
these on the phone: "When you leave in the morning,
you never know if you'll return." Lost in water,
blood falters; then swirled to roses, it salts the slaughter.

After the August Wedding
in Lahore, Pakistan,

we all—Save the couple!—returned to pain,
some in Massachusetts, some in Kashmir
where, wet by turns, Order's dry campaign
had glued petals with bullets to each pane—
Sarajevo Roses! A gift to glass,
that city's name. What else breaks? A lover's pain!
But happiness? Must it, too, bring pain?
Question I may ask because of a night—
by ice-sculptures, all my words sylvanite
under one gaze that filled my glass with pain.
That thirst haunts as does the fevered dancing,
flames dying among orchids flown in from Sing-

apore! Sing then, not of the promising
but the Promised End. Of what final pain,
what image of that horror can I sing?
To be forgotten the most menacing!
Those "Houseboat Days in the Vale of Kashmir,"
for instance, in '29: Did they sing
just of love then, or was love witnessing
its departure for other thirsts—the glass
of Dal Lake ruffled half by "Satin Glass,"
that chandeliered boat barely focusing
on emptiness—last half of any night?
In Lahore the chanteuse crooned "Stop the Night"—

the groom's request—after the banquet. *Night,
that Empress, is here, your bride. She will sing!
Her limbs break like chrysanthemums. O Night,*

what hints have been passed in the sky tonight?
The stars so quiet, what galaxies of pain
leave them unable to prophesy this night?
With a rending encore, she closed the night.
There was, like this, long ago in Kashmir,
a moment—after a concert—outside Kashmir
Book Shop that left me stranded, by midnight,
in a hotel mirror. Would someone glass
me in—from what? Filled, I emptied my glass,

lured by a stranger's eyes into their glass.
There, nothing melted, as in Lahore's night:
Heat had brought sweat to the lip of my glass
but sculptures kept iced their aberrant glass.
To be forgotten my most menacing
image of the End—expelled from the glass
of someone's eyes as if no full-length glass
had held us, safe, from political storms? Pain,
then, becomes love's thirst—the ultimate pain
to lose a stranger! O, to have said, glass
in hand, "Where Thou art—that—is Home— / Cashmere—
or Calvary—the same"! In the Cašmir

and Poison and Brut air, my rare Cashmere
thrown off, the stranger knew my arms are glass,
that banished from Eden (on earth: Kashmir)
into the care of storms (it rains in Kashmir,
in Lahore, and here in Amherst tonight),
in each new body I would drown Kashmir.

A brigadier says, *The boys of Kashmir*
break so quickly, we make their bodies sing,
on the rack, till no song is left to sing.
"Butterflies pause / On their passage Cashmere—"
And happiness: must it only bring pain?
The century is ending. It is pain

from which love departs into all new pain:
Freedom's terrible thirst, flooding Kashmir,
is bringing love to its tormented glass.
Stranger, who will inherit the last night
of the past? Of what shall I not sing, and sing?

(for Shafaq Husain)

ROOMS ARE NEVER
FINISHED

I pray you, oh, I pray: Don't die.
I'm here, alone, with you, in a future April . . .
—PIER PAOLO PASOLINI, "Prayer to my Mother"

On the shore where Time casts up its stray
wreckage, we gather corks and broken planks,
whence much indeed may be argued and more
guessed; but what the great ship was that
has gone down into the deep that
we shall never see.
—ANONYMOUS

To a home at war, my father, siblings, and I brought my mother's body for burial. It was the only thing to do, for she had longed for home throughout her illness. In 1990, Kashmir—the cause of hostility between India and Pakistan since their creation in 1947—erupted into a full-scale uprising for self-determination. The resulting devastation—large-scale atrocities and the death, by some accounts, of 70,000 people—has led to despair and rage, then only rage, then only despair. Because both countries are nuclear powers now, international anxiety has increased: Kashmir, it is feared, may be the flashpoint of a nuclear war. The ongoing catastrophe—the focus of *The Country Without a Post Office*, my previous volume of poems—provides the backdrop to this volume. In January 1996 my mother came to the States for treatment of brain cancer. Till her death—in a hospital in Northampton, Massachusetts, on 27 April 1997—we were with her at my brother's home in Amherst.

Lenox Hill

(In Lenox Hill Hospital, after surgery, my
mother said the sirens sounded like the
elephants of Mihiragula when his men drove
them off cliffs in the Pir Panjal Range.)

The Hun so loved the cry, one falling elephant's,
he wished to hear it again. At dawn, my mother
heard, in her hospital-dream of elephants,
sirens wail through Manhattan like elephants
forced off Pir Panjal's rock cliffs in Kashmir:
the soldiers, so ruled, had rushed the elephants.
The greatest of all footprints is the elephant's,
said the Buddha. But not lifted from the universe,
those prints vanished forever into the universe,
though nomads still break news of those elephants
as if it were just yesterday the air spread the dye
("War's annals will fade into night / Ere their story die"),

the punishing khaki whereby the world sees us die
out, mourning you, O massacred elephants!
Months later, in Amherst, she dreamt: She was, with dia-
monds, being stoned to death. I prayed: If she must die,
let it only be some dream. But there were times, Mother,
while you slept, that I prayed, "Saints, let her die."
Not, I swear by you, that I wished you to die
but to save you as you were, young, in song in Kashmir,
and I, one festival, crowned Krishna by you, Kashmir
listening to my flute. You never let gods die.
Thus I swear, here and now, not to forgive the universe
that would let me get used to a universe

without you. She, she alone, was the universe
as she earned, like a galaxy, her right not to die,
defying the Merciful of the Universe,

Master of Disease, "in the circle of her traverse"
of drug-bound time. And where was the god of elephants,
plump with Fate, when tusk to tusk, the universe,
dyed green, became ivory? Then let the universe,
like Paradise, be considered a tomb. Mother,
they asked me, *So how's the writing?* I answered *My mother
is my poem.* What did they expect? For no verse
sufficed except the promise, fading, of Kashmir
and the cries that reached you from the cliffs of Kashmir

(across fifteen centuries) in the hospital. *Kashmir,
she's dying!* How her breathing drowns out the universe
as she sleeps in Amherst. Windows open on Kashmir:
There, the fragile wood-shrines—so far away—of Kashmir!
O Destroyer, let her return there, if just to die.
Save the right she gave its earth to cover her, Kashmir
has no rights. When the windows close on Kashmir,
I see the blizzard-fall of ghost-elephants.
I hold back—she couldn't bear it—one elephant's
story: his return (in a country far from Kashmir)
to the jungle where each year, on the day his mother
died, he touches with his trunk the bones of his mother.

"As you sit here by me, you're just like my mother,"
she tells me. I imagine her: a bride in Kashmir,
she's watching, at the Regal, her first film with Father.
If only I could gather you in my arms, Mother,
I'd save you—now my daughter—from God. The universe
opens its ledger. I write: How helpless was God's mother!

Each page is turned to enter grief's accounts. Mother,
I see a hand. *Tell me it's not God's.* Let it die.
I see it. It's filling with diamonds. Please let it die.
Are you somewhere, alive, somewhere alive, Mother?
Do you hear what I once held back: in one elephant's
cry, by his mother's bones, the cries of those elephants

that stunned the abyss? Ivory blots out the elephants.
I enter this: *The Belovéd leaves one behind to die.*
For compared to my grief for you, what are those of Kashmir,
and what (I close the ledger) are the griefs of the universe
when I remember you—beyond all accounting—O my mother?

From Amherst to Kashmir

1. Karbala: A History of the "House of Sorrow"

In a distant age and climate, the tragic scene
of the death of Husayn will awaken the sympathy
of the coldest reader.
— EDWARD GIBBON

Jesus and his disciples, passing through the plain of Karbala, saw "a herd of gazelles, crowding together and weeping." Astonished, the disciples looked at their Lord. He spoke: "At this site the grandson of Prophet Muhammad (Peace be upon him) will one day be killed." And Jesus wept. *Oh, that my head were waters, and mine eyes a fountain of tears, that I might weep day and night for the slain* . . . And Jesus wept. And as if the news has just reached them — fourteen hundred years after the Battle of Karbala (near ancient Babylon, not far from the Euphrates) in the year A.H. 61/A.D. 680 — mourners weep for "the prince among martyrs," Hussain, grandson of the Prophet and son of Ali ("Father of Clay") and Fatima (the Prophet's only surviving child). Memorializing Hussain on the tenth of Muharram (*Ashura*) is *the* rite of Shi'a Islam — so central that at funerals those events are woven into elegies, every death framed by that "Calvary." For just "as Jesus went to Jerusalem to die on the cross," Hussain "went to Karbala to accept the passion that had been meant for him from the beginning of time."

. . .

From the beginning of time? When Ishmael was saved, did the ram suffice, even though Gabriel had brought it from Paradise, from the very presence of God? Because both father as the slayer and son as the victim had submitted to His will, God called out, "Abraham, you have fulfilled the vision." And He ransomed Ishmael with a "great redeeming sacrifice"—completed only centuries later on the battlefield that became the altar. Abraham foreknew all and wept bitterly. God spoke: "Abraham, through your grief for Hussain, I have ransomed your grief for your son as though you had slain him with your own hand."

. . .

At the call of the people of Kufa (their hearts were with him, their swords with his enemies), Hussain, with his family and supporters, set out from Mecca, "along the pilgrim route across the desert of central Arabia," to challenge the tyranny of the Caliph Yazid. In Karbala their caravan (2 Muharram 61/2 October 680) was intercepted by Yazid's troops under Obeidullah. Till the tenth of Muharram, they withstood the siege, choosing death, not surrender. Prevented from reaching the Euphrates, for three days before the massacre they were without water. Anguished by the children's cries, Abbas, Hussain's half brother, led a daring sortie to fill a few waterskins but he perished.

. . .

On 9 Muharram, as if putting on his own shroud, Hussain spoke: "Tomorrow our end will come. I ask you to go away to safety. I free you, I do not hold you back. Night will give you a cover; use it as a steed." He had the lights turned out. Fewer than one hundred remained—among them the women, the children, the old.

. . .

And the borrowed night ends. They line up before the army. The rear of the tents is protected by wood and reeds set on fire. The first arrows come, in a shower. Hussain's nephew Qasim is struck and dies in his uncle's arms. Every man is killed. The women look on in terror. Alone, Hussain returns to the tents to console the children and women, among them his sister Zainab, and bids them farewell. At sunset, the soldiers turn to pillage. The bodies are decapitated, stripped of all covering. Hussain's severed head is brought to Obeidullah. He carelessly turns it over with his staff. "Gently," one officer protests. "By Allah! I have seen those lips kissed by the blessed mouth of Muhammad."

. . .

The morning of 12 Muharram saw seventy-two heads raised on lances, each held by a soldier, followed by the women on camels. One of Hussain's sons, the only male survivor, had lain sick during battle. The "adornment of God's servants," he was saved when Zainab threw herself over him. At the sight of the decapitated bodies, the women's lamentations rose: "O Muhammad! The angels of Heaven send blessings upon you, but this is your Hussain, so humiliated and disgraced, covered with blood and cut into pieces, and your daughters are made captives, your butchered family is left for the East Wind to cover with dust!" The head of Hussain was put on display in Kufa before it was sent to Yazid. Held in a dungeon, the captives before long were taken to Damascus.

. . .

Mourners beg for water—the martyrs' thirst. They wound their heads, and "the green grassy field" where their processions end "becomes bloodied and looks like a field of poppies." *And my brother knows he will die. He has himself put on his shroud.* A deluge of weeping follows. So I remember, since childhood. One *majlis** stays—Summer 1992—when for two years Death had turned every day in Kashmir into some family's Karbala. We celebrated *Ashura* with relatives, in the afternoon—because of night curfew. That evening, at home, my mother was suddenly in tears. I was puzzled, then very moved: Since she was a girl she had felt Zainab's grief as her own.

. . .

At my mother's funeral a mourner sang one of her favorite Kashmiri elegies, given to Zainab, in which her exile is nearly unbearable. Those words now are my mother's, for she too was tired, fighting death, from hospital to hospital, from city to city.

2. Zainab's Lament in Damascus

Over Hussain's mansion what night has fallen?

Look at me, O people of Shaam,** the Prophet's
only daughter's daughter, his only child's child.

---

* *majlis*: A gathering of people, specifically to mourn Karbala.
** Shaam: Arabic word for Syria.

Over my brother's
bleeding mansion dawn rose—at such forever
cost?

    So weep now, you who of passion never
made a holocaust, for I saw his children
slain in the desert,
crying for water.

        Hear me. Remember Hussain,
what he gave in Karbala, he the severed
heart, the very heart of Muhammad, left there
bleeding, unburied.

Deaf Damascus, here in your Caliph's dungeons
where they mock the blood of your Prophet, I'm an
orphan, Hussain's sister, a tyrant's prisoner.

Father of Clay, he
cried, *forgive me. Syria triumphs, orphans
all your children. Farewell.*

            And then he wore his
shroud of words and left us alone forever.

Paradise, hear me—
On my brother's body what night has fallen?

Let the rooms of Heaven be deafened, Angels,
with my unheard cry in the Caliph's palace:

Syria hear me

Over Hussain's mansion what night has fallen

I alone am left to tell my brother's story

On my brother's body what dawn has risen

Weep for my brother
World, weep for Hussain

3. Summers of Translation

> *Desolation's desert. I'm here with shadows*
> *of your voice . . .*
> — FAIZ AHMED FAIZ, "Memory"

"Memory" — two years after your death they tell me — has
no translation. We knew it in a loved version,
the words languidly climbed by a singer of Faiz,

and, of course, we knew it well in the desolation
mastered by singers on Radio Pakistan
slowly-slowly . . . with shadows.
                      But it's a *bhajan**

from a black and white film, sung to a dark icon,
that I recall—the story, from every angle, bleak
(Dark blue god don't cast me into oblivion,

in the temples, all your worshippers are asleep):
As you told it, the child-bride would die, and the rain,
you remembered as a girl, would come each dawn to keep

her from what you longed for her. With thunder, a train—
from Pakistan?—would crash and bring down the refrain,
and your tears. The train's whistle, years later, would rend
the heart.
      As I begin "Memory" all by myself
(I'll hold on to your sleeve, blue god, till the end),

so many summers, so many monsoons, dimmed on Time's shelf,
return, framed by the voice you gave to each story,
as when—in the last summer of peace—the heart itself

* *bhajan*: Hindu devotional song.

256

was the focus: you read all of Faiz aloud to me:
we chose poems that would translate best. So strange:
Why did we not linger just a bit on "Memory"?

It was '89, the stones were not far, signs of change
everywhere (Kashmir would soon be in literal
flames). Well, our dawns were so perfectly set to arrange

our evenings in color that liberty with each ghazal
was my only way of being loyal to any original . . .

I shelve "Memory" to hear Begum Akhtar* enclose —
in Raga *Jogia* ** — the wound-cry of the gazelle:
"Not all, no, only a few return as the rose

or the tulip." That ghazal held under her spell.
But when you welcomed me in later summers to Kashmir,
every headline read:
                    PARADISE ON EARTH BECOMES HELL.

The night was broken in two by the Call to Prayer
which found nothing to steal but my utter disbelief.
In every home, although Muharram was not yet here,

* Begum Akhtar: One of India's great singers, and the greatest ghazal singer of all time.
** *Jogia*: Among the more austere ragas.

Zainab wailed. Only Karbala could frame our grief:
The wail rose: *How could such a night fall on Hussain?*
Mother, you remembered perfectly that *God is a thief*

when memory is a black and white film again
(*Dark Krishna,*
         don't let your Radha die in the rain*):

You wait, at the end of Memory, with what befell
Zainab—
         from Karbala to Kufa to Damascus.
You are wearing black. The cry of the gazelle

fills the night. It is Zainab's cry. You cry it for us
so purely that even in memory it lets memory cease.
For your voice could make any story so various,

so new, that even terrible pain would decrease
into wonder. But for me, I who of passion
always make a holocaust, will there be a summer of peace?

A mother dies. There's a son's execution.
On Memory's mantle—where summers may truly shine—
all, as never before, is nothing but translation.

* Radha: Consort of Krishna.

It is Muharram again.

     Of God there is no sign.

Mother,

  you are "the breath drawn after every line."

4. Above the Cities

> *God is the Light of the heavens and the earth —*
> *the likeness of His light is as a niche wherein*
> *is a lamp . . .*
>   —THE KORAN, Surah 24:35

Boston-Frankfurt-Delhi. Lufthansa airborne,
coffin-holding coffin. Now home to Kashmir.
Was it prophesied what we, broken, gather?
She is with us and

we—without her? Where is the lamp that's "kindled
from a Blesséd Tree," that one olive which is
"neither of the East nor the West whose oil would
well-nigh keep shining

though untouched by fire"? For

> *Doomsday but barely had taken its first breath*
> *when I remembered again the hour you left,*

Doomsday's very
first breath—which was but your departure—that I
learn by heart again and again. I'm piling
Doomsday on Doomsday

over oceans, continents, deserts, cities.
Airport after airport, the plane is darkness
plunged into the sunrise,

For I had also seen the moth rush to the candle—
then nothing but the wrenched flame gasping in knots.

So nothing then but
Karbala's slaughter

through my mother's eyes at the *majlis*, mourning
Zainab in the Damascene court, for she must
stand before the Caliph alone, her eyes my
mother's, my mother's

hers across these centuries, each year black-robed
in that 1992 Kashmir summer—
evening curfew minutes away: The sun died.
We had with Zainab's

words returned home:

Hussain, I'm in exile from exile, lost from
city to city.

Outside, the guns were punctual
stars. The night was Muharram's orphan-vigil,
she in sudden tears. "Mummy, what's the matter?"
"Nothing, it's Zainab's

grief, that's all." Her eyes are two candles darkened
with laments found lost on our lips,

Over Hussain's mansion what night is falling?

two candles
lit above the cities she'll never visit,
names that were spellbound

on her lips, their magic unbearable now —
Naples, Athens, Isfahan, Kashgar. Hush. For
over Hussain's mansion the night that's dropped is
leading the heart in

one jade line unbroken to Doomsday: *She is
gone!* —the nurse's words. And again the flat line
(*She is gone!*), for in the ICU green, the
monitor's pulse was

but the heart unable to empty itself.

O bleeding mansion, what night has fallen?

She is gone! Now out of the cabin's blue dark,
blinding lights accompany *We'll be landing*
shortly at Delhi

Airport—city of my birth! Our descent is
just her voice (I'd crushed the dawn tablets into
spoons of water): *You must now write my story,*
Bhaiya, * *my story*

only. On the shelf you're deluged with night-veiled
light, your face in that niche where memory, Mother,
darkens with the Light of the heavens.

 Zainab weeps for Hussain in Karbala's night.

      Still it's
easy to write your

story—you are even in lines in which you
can't be found. It's easy to write your story.
For whatever city I fly to, even
that of my birth, you

aren't there to welcome me. And any city
I am leaving—even if one you've never
seen—my parting words are for you alone. For
where there is farewell,

 * Bhaiya: The author's pet name.

262

you are there. And where there's a son, in any
language saying *Adieu* to his mother, she is
you and that son *(There by the gate)* is me, that
son is me. Always.

5. Memory

from Faiz Ahmed Faiz

Desolation's desert. I'm here with shadows
of your voice, your lips as mirage, now trembling.
Grass and dust of distance have let this desert
bloom with your roses.

Near me breathes the air that's your kiss. It smoulders,
slowly-slowly, musk of itself. And farther,
drop by drop, beyond the horizon, shines the
dew of your lit face.

Memory's placed its hand so on Time's face, touched it
so caressingly that although it's still our
parting's morning, it's as if night's come, bringing
you to my bare arms.

6. New Delhi Airport

Whom the flame itself has gone searching for,
that moth — just imagine!
    — Bombay film song

Haze of April heat. We are on the tarmac.
Soon a journey's end will begin — and soon end.
How she longed for home, to return alive, go
home to light candles . . .

All the flames have severed themselves from candles,
darkened Kashmir's shrines to go find their lost one,
burning God the Moth in stray blasphemy. His
Wings have caught fire,

lit up broken idols in temples, on whom
Scripture breaks, breaks down to confess His violence:
what their breaking's cost the forsaken nation
that now awaits her

at the wind- and water-stretched end of Earth — to
which, veiled, she's being brought back from Goodbye's other
sky, the God-stretched end of the blue, returning
as the Belovéd,

final lonely rival to God. The flames, like
moths, look just for her. Will they, searching Kashmir,
be extinguished, longing for her and prophets?
All of a sudden

through the haze the crated shrine's taken past us.
When it's gone, I know she was trying to tell me—
what? For veiled, her voice is the veil itself. *O
Father of Clay, your*

*daughter Zainab wanders in thirst. The Prophet's
blood is streams on Karbala's sands. What truth's here?
Hussain's dead and she's caught in exile, lost from
city to city.*

Pilgrims brought back clay from that site of slaughter—
Karbala was chosen for Kashmir's seasons,
mixed into the graveyard's cold beds of roses.
We are such pilgrims

too, returning thus with her shrine. It enters
first the hold's, then memory's desolation.
Soon we climb the ramp, and the sky is empty
once we are airborne.

7. Film *Bhajan* Found on a 78 RPM

Dark god shine on me you're all I have left
nothing else blue god you are all I have
I won't let go I'll cling on to your robe

I am yours your Radha my bangles break
I break my bangles my heart is glass come back
blue god there's nothing you are all I have

let there be no legend of a lost one
who breaks her bangles who lets herself die
who says you hid yourself to break my heart

your eyes are my refuge hide me from the world
dark god Dark Krishna you are all I have
do not hide yourself merely to break my heart

all day I'm restless all night I can't sleep
the morning star sinks it drowns in my eyes
the night is heavy its dark is iron

take my hand place your hands in mine in yours
I'm yours dark god do not abandon me
all night I won't sleep even for a while

in the temples all the worshippers sleep
your flute strikes the stars its legends echo
and the soul in its trance crosses the sky

my heart keeps breaking does not stop breaking
it says dark god I will never leave you
the heart is awake it keeps on breaking

all night I'm awake I'll keep you awake
take this vow that I am yours I am yours
dark god you are all I have all I have

all night I'm awake I'll keep you awake
in your temples all the worshippers sleep
only swear I am yours that I am yours

only take this vow I am yours dark god
dark god you are all you are all I have
swear only swear I am yours I am yours

8. Srinagar Airport

There is no god but God.
—THE KORAN

Only clouds. The rain has just stopped. And as her
shrine is onto Srinagar's tarmac lowered,
listen: Even they are here speechless, weeping,
those who of passion

never made a holocaust. One by one, they
hold me in their arms: *How could this have happened,
Bhaiya, how could it?* To the waiting van she's
brought on their shoulders.

Who are all these strangers for whom she rivals
God today? They stare. And we speed through streets that
follow *Farewell Farewell* and then at each turn
go into hiding —

for each turn's a world that recalls her, every
turn her world unable to say Goodbye, though
she, from every corner, is waving with such
pity we melt, melt

past the world she loved, past each corner she is
waving from, just waving herself goodbye. Who
doesn't owe her tears when we reach home and her
house — it is *her* house —

echoes with her keys? The doors open — she is
everywhere. Yes, here it must start, the FAREWELL,
from this very room, from its quiet center.
Outside, a man says,

"Soon it will be dark. We must reach the graveyard."
From the garden, echo to echo, voices
rise. "We must . . ." The afternoon darkens. She is
farther than any

god today and nearer than any god. And
God? He's farther, farther from us, forever
far. We lift the shrine. The women break into
There is no god but

9. *God*

"In the Name of the Merciful" let night begin.
I must light lamps without her—at every shrine?
God then is only the final assassin.

The prayers end. Emptiness waits to take her in.
With laments found lost on my lips, I resign
myself to His every Name. Let night begin

without any light, for as they carry the coffin
from the mosque to the earth, no stars shine
to reveal Him as only the final assassin.

The mourners, at the dug earth's every margin,
fill emptiness with their hands. Their eyes meet mine
when with no Name of His I let my night begin.

In the dark the marble of each tomb grows skin.
I tear it off. I make a holocaust. I underline
God is the only, the only assassin

as flames put themselves out, at once, on her shrine
(they have arrived like moths from temples and mosques).
In no one's name but hers I let night begin.

10. Ghalib's Ghazal[*]

Not all, only a few —
    disguised as tulips, as roses —
        return from ashes.
What possibilities
    has the earth forever
        covered, what faces?

Time ago I too could recall
    those moon-lit nights,
        wine on the Saqi's[**] roof—
But Time's shelved them now
    in its niche, in
        Memory's dim places.

Let me weep, let this blood
    flow from my eyes.
        She is leaving.

   [*] Ghalib: He is to Urdu what Shakespeare is to English, Dante to Italian,
and Pushkin to Russian.
    [**] Saqi: One who pours wine.

These tears, I'll say, have
        lit my eyes, two candles
                for love's darkest spaces.

What isn't his?
        He is Sleep, is Peace, is Night,
                mere mortal become god
when your hair lies scattered,
        shining, on his shoulder,
                he now one whom nothing effaces.

Wine, a giver of life! Hold the glass.
        The palm's lines, as one, will
                rush to life —
Here's my hand, its
        life-line beating, here
                Look! the glass it raises.

Man is numbed to pain
        when he's sorrow-beaten.
                Sorrows, piled up, ease pain.
Grief crushed me so
        again and again it became
                the pain that pain erases.

World, take note, should Ghalib
  keep weeping, you'll see
    only a wilderness
where you built
  your terraced cities,
    your marble palaces.

11. The Fourth Day*

> *Doomsday had but — but barely had — breathed its first*
> *when I again remembered you as you were leaving.*
>   — GHALIB

The dead — so quickly — become the poor at night.

And the poor? They are the dead so soon by night . . .

But whom the news has reached in the Valley of Death

(The Belovéd is gone The Belovéd is gone)

they are not the dead, they are the poor at dawn,

they who have come from shrines after breaking their heads on the
  threshold-stones of God.

* The Fourth Day: Among Muslims, it marks the end of the first active
period of mourning.

. . .

When you left flames deserted their wicks in the shrines.

Now they arrive with the poor to light up the few who have
   returned from ashes, disguised as roses.

What possibilities the earth has forever covered, what faces?

They have arrived with wings, as burning moths, to put themselves
   out on your grave.

From behind headstones they keep coming with the dead — who are
   not the dead —

just the poor, wrapped in blankets, risen at dawn, walking like the
   dead by the wrecked river . . .

From behind headstones they keep coming toward us, silent on a
   carpet by your grave.

They are not the dead. We are the poor at dawn.

When the flames are wrenched, gasping in knots, they are not the
   dead. We are the poor at dawn.

And when the flames die, they leave what is left of their hands.

In fingerprints they leave all their prayers on your grave.

. . .

Four days: And eternities have so quickly slowed down.

Only a few —disguised as roses —return from ashes.

They are the poor, not the dead at dawn, who have come to weep
    with all their passion:

Doomsday barely begins when it repeats its beginning

(For what is Doomsday but the Belovéd's departure?)

and I again remember you leaving with the caravan of dawn.

Four days have passed. Eternities have slowed down:

See, see where Hussain's blood streams the sands.

They are not the dead, we are the poor at dawn.

I stood weeping in the desert and the sun rose.

And the sun fell on the roofs of the poor. And it fell on mansions in
    the mountains.

Again I see you leave with the caravan of dawn.

Doomsday begins. It keeps on beginning.

And the Belovéd leaves one behind to die.

. . .

The sun has barely risen. They await us in the mosque.

We leave you alone; we leave the earth to you.

In the courtyard they are gathered. There's only Karbala in their
hearts.

And Abraham weeps. And God's angels weep.

And the sun still beats in the desert:

See, see where Hussain's blood streams the desert.

And God's angels weep. And Jesus weeps.

The Belovéd leaves one behind to die.

And with the wounded gazelle's wail in his heart (It is Zainab's cry,
It is Zainab's cry), an old man begins:

"Over Hussain's mansion what night has fallen . . ."

12. By the Waters of the Sind

Is the sinking moon like a prisoner
    sentenced somewhere to Black Water,
perhaps left hanged on the horizon
of an Andaman island? But here,
    in Kashmir, by these waters,
its light will leave me—where?

My father is—in Persian—reciting
    Hafiz of Shiraz, that "Nothing
in this world is without terrible
barriers— / Except love, but only when
    it begins." And the host fills
everyone's glass again.

So what is separation's geography?
    Everything is just that mystery,
everything is this roar that deafens:
this stream has branched off from the Indus,
    in Little Tibet, just to
find itself where Porus

miles down (there it will join the Jhelum)
    lost to the Greeks. It will become,
in Pakistan, the Indus again.
Leaning against the Himalayas
    (the mountains here are never
in the distance), wine-glass

in hand, I see evening come on. It is
   two months since you left us. So this
is separation? Sharpened against
rocks, the stream, rapid-cutting the night,
   finds its steel a little stained
with the beginning light,

and the moon must rise now from behind
   that one pine-topped mountain to find
us without you. I stare at one guest
who is asking Father to fill them
   in on—what else?—the future,
burnishing that dark gem

of Kashmir with a history of saints, with
   prophecy, with kings, and with myth,
and I want them to change the subject
to these waters that must already
   be silver there where the moon
sees the Indus empty

itself into the Arabian Sea. What
   rustle of trees the wind forgot
reaches me through this roar as the moon,
risen completely, silvers the world
   so ruthlessly, shining on
me a terror so pearled

that *How dare the moon* — I want to cry out,
   Mother — *shine so hauntingly out*
here when I've sentenced it to black waves
inside me? Why has it not perished?
   How dare it shine on an earth
from which you have vanished?

Rooms Are Never Finished

Many of my favorite things are broken.
— MARIO BUATTA, interior designer
known as "The King of Chintz"

In here it's deliberately dark so one may sigh

in peace. Please come in. How long has it been?
Upstairs — climb slowly — the touch is more certain.
You've been, they say, everywhere. What city's left?
I've brought the world indoors. One wants certainty.
Not in art — well, you've hardly changed — but, why,

in life. But for small invisible hands, no wall
would be lacquered a rain forest's colors. Before,
these walls had just mirrors (I tried on — for size —
kismet's barest air). Remember? You were
led through all the spare rooms I was to die

in. But look how each room's been refurbished:
This screen in stitches silk-routes a river
down Asia, past laughing Buddhas, China
a lantern burning burning burning for
"God to aggrandise, God to glorify"

in (How one passes through such thick walls!).
Candles float past inked-in laborers
but for whose hands this story would be empty,
rooms where one plots only to die, nothing
Dear! but a bare flame for you to come by

in. *Don't touch that vase!* Long ago
its waist, abandoned by scrolling foliage,
was banded by hands, banded quick with omens:
a galloping flood, hooves iron by the river's edge.
O beating night, what could have reined the sky

in? Come to the window: panes plot the earth
apart. In the moon's crush, the cobalt stars
shed light—blue—on Russia: the republics porcelain,
the Urals mezzotint. Why are you weeping,
dear friend? Hush, rare guest. Once a passer-by

in tears, his footsteps dying, was . . . well, I rushed
out and he was gone. Out there it's poison.
Out there one longs for all one's ever bought,
for shades that lighten a scene: When the last leaves
were birds spent wingless on trees, love, the cage to cry

in, was glass-stormed by the North. Now that God
is news, what's left but prayer, and . . . well, if you
love something, why argue? What we own betters
any tale of God's—no? That framed scroll downstairs
and here! this shell drowned men heard God's reply

in. Listen, my friend. But for quick hands, my walls
would be mirrors. A house? A work in progress,
always. But: Could love's season be more than this?
I'll wipe your tears. Turn to me. My world would be
mere mirrors cut to multiply, then multiply

in. But for small hands. Invisible. Quick . . .

(for Mathew Stadler)

Ghazal

What will suffice for a true-love knot? Even the rain?
But he has bought grief's lottery, bought even the rain.

"our glosses / wanting in this world" "Can you remember?"
Anyone! when we thought the lovers taught even the rain?

After we died — *That was it!* — God left us in the dark.
And as we forgot the dark, we forgot even the rain.

Drought was over. Where was I? Drinks were on the house.
For mixers, my love, you'd poured — what? — even the rain.

Of this pear-shaped orange's perfumed twist, I will say:
Extract Vermouth from the bergamot, even the rain.

How did the Enemy love you — with earth? air? and fire?
He held just one thing back till he got even: the rain.

This is God's site for a new house of executions?
You swear by the Bible, Despot, even the rain?

After the bones — those flowers — this was found in the urn:
The lost river, ashes from the ghat, even the rain.

What was I to prophesy if not the end of the world?
A salt pillar for the lonely lot, even the rain.

How the air raged, desperate, streaming the earth with flames —
to help burn down my house, Fire sought even the rain.

He would raze the mountains, he would level the waves;
he would, to smooth his epic plot, even the rain.

New York belongs at daybreak to only me, just me —
to make this claim Memory's brought even the rain.

They've found the knife that killed you, but whose prints are these?
No one has such small hands, Shahid, not even the rain.

Barcelona Airport

Are you carrying anything that could
be dangerous for the other passengers?

O just my heart   first terrorist
(a flame dies by dawn   in every shade)

Crescent-lit   it fits the profile
on your screen

          Damascene-green
in blood's mansions   (candle that burned
till its flame died   in blue corridors)

it's relit each time   it tries to exit
this body for another's   in another century

(Andalusia was   but to be missed)

Last week I went   to the Pyrenees
and then came here   for the year's farewell
to your city

          In your custom of countdowns
as the gongs were struck   I gulped each grape
(the heart skipped   its beats wildly):

Ten . . . Seven   the Year whirled in
to castanets   to strings DRUMS Two

DRUMS *ONE!*   DRUMS *Champagne!*

So what white   will the heart wear
till the soul is   its own blood-filled crystal
ruby refuge   for a fugitive angel?

His wings waxed silver   to track the Atlantic
he won't—like   any body—let

the soul go   So delete my emerald beats
(in each color all night   a candle burns)

Hit ENTER   the Mediterranean
this minute   is uncut sapphire

And your Catalan sky?   Behold how to hide
one must . . . like God   spend all one's blue

(for Rafiq Kathwari)

A Secular Comedy

1. Heaven

Heaven's lovesick Mediterranean blue
paper (parchment thickened to sky to hide His
loneliness) now peels to reveal what's left of
all that was Heaven.

I, Earth's ghost, am here where the windows, broken,
still reveal that He has learned nothing from His
errors, clouds in cobwebs on ceilings, shredded
wings in the corners.

"Vanished days, how," Gabriel says, "we miss them."
Drink, for even God shall not remain. Satan's
voice? His voice preserved here till now? And perfect?
Who'd dare sing after

such a bitter melody? God is voiceless,
missing passion. All of His hands lie broken.
This is death? This fire of separation?
This is survival?

Songs I know! What unfinished pain that leads to
ghosts has brought me here, what unfinished business?
Empty, only wilderness veined inside me,
I, with no shadow?

Even You don't give me a shadow: Your Light—
all the lights of Heaven—are dimmed tonight. Is
this the anniversary—Love's expulsion—
Night of the Fallen

Angels? Who will sing now? Was there just poison
or some grief in You when he fell through Chaos—
Your Abyss—for nights, and his mad wings, raging,
deafened the soundproof

halls of Heaven? What is apart from legend?
But He doesn't answer. He lets His Light go
out completely. And I am left without a
chance of a shadow.

2. Earth

Sudden god, his head's on my melting shoulder:
gap in nature: Oregon: evening taxi:
neon-slow from . . . downtown to . . . Jantzen Beach where
sleep will abandon

night in rose-lit Doubletree's quiet lobby,
silence ripe for worship, the hour that's taken:
Over me he's pulling down Heaven. Will he
after my body

hear hearts breaking breaking in rooms he passes?
Every door awaits a returning lover,
corridors caught gleaming with wounds, the story
(Violence's) no one

tells going on and on. In a time like this one
stars are shredded. Who will decipher grief then?
Grief's the question asked as the given answer:
Grief is the answer,

midnight shot with pearls: like his gaze that rushes
toward me, the rapids of separation
whirling loud, my face held below the water-
fall of his time. He's

leaving? No, he's settling on me his gaze now,
entering my sleep. What remains of night he
owns, and he's its message to me, awake, his
hair on my shoulder.

3. Hell

Hell, then! Pandemonium's walls have diamonds.
We who lost our lovers on earth are welcome;
all are welcome, mirrored among the angels
lonely with pity.

Pity? Yes, for Heaven (To us what music,
we *who trade in love*) and for love's first story:
God and Satan—*Iblis*, first monotheist,
jealously guarding

God as only he could have known Him. "God's so
lonely . . . else would He," asks one fallen angel,
emphasizing *lonely*, "else would He, *would* He
punish man so? For

none of you can understand Him." Sorry,
now for God, and full of such longing myself
while on Earth he's missed in his ruined temples,
what can I do but

stare at sky-sized posters of God in mirrors?
Archived here, these stolen reflections, kisses
pressed on guarded tablets of Heaven's chipped Word,
numbered and signed by

God—and *him?* "Please tell us," the angels beg him.
Kiss and tell? Will that suit this devil-lover?
Framed in every mirror, now really smiling,
bevelled sapphire,

God to me is closer, he shrugs his shoulders,
than the jugular is to man, so even
now, bereft of love, I must guard God's secrets.
Call it perverse or—

"—What?" the angels, taking their wings off lightly, say. "*It's simpler*," he interrupts, "*it's that. . . . Well, come and try*" —he's pouring some wine —"*this vintage aged here in cellars,*

Heaven's ruby. Under my wings I hid some bottles just before I was pushed through exits, breaking panes. What lovely reminder, this wine, of that passion —

Heaven's nights, His blood, then His flesh, my open wings that tightly closed to again be opened . . . Stop. I must. This hour, my Belovéd Tyrant surely is weeping."

The Nature of Temporal Order

from Alexander Pushkin (1799–1837)

Rites of iron—hour of the Crucifixion:
Magdalene is mute in the Tree's forgiving
shade, and in the sun, on the other side, the
Virgin. In epic

griefs, both Marys witness their one God nailed to
Life, His slow torment. And the Celebration's
carried out: They vanish, both women, unseen;
quick, in their place, two

sentries, ruthless, stand at the Cross's foot, as
if they guard the gates of the Viceroy's mansion.
Has the State then seized as its effects even
God and His sacred

blood—not just the nails and the wood? Please tell me
why you're here—to save Him from scavengers and
thieves? You broke His flesh, with your thorns you crowned Him.
Guards, let the reason

you've been sent be clearer. To sanctify Him,
He whose blood is wine, its astonished moment?
Or, more puzzling, faith has bewildered Order:
Could you be thinking

Adam's lost sons—tribe whom His Execution
saved—insult Him by their mere presence and must be
kept far? Or: It's simpler? You follow orders
so the Empire's

lords and ladies—tourists from Rome—may marvel
that the king of kings is their Caesar's captive,
hanged man they unhindered must watch as they on
Calvary stroll by.

Ghazal

Feel the patient's heart
Pounding —oh please, this once —
   —JAMES MERRILL

I'll do what I must if I'm bold in real time.
A refugee, I'll be paroled in real time.

Cool evidence clawed off like shirts of hell-fire?
A former existence untold in real time . . .

The one you would choose: were you led then by him?
What longing, O *Yaar*,* is controlled in real time?

Each syllable sucked under waves of our earth—
The funeral love comes to hold in real time!

They left him alive so that he could be lonely—
The god of small things is not consoled in real time.

Please afterwards empty my pockets of keys—
It's hell in the city of gold in real time.

God's angels again are—for Satan!—forlorn.
Salvation was bought but sin sold in real time.

And who is the terrorist, who the victim?
We'll know if the country is polled in real time.

"Behind a door marked DANGER" are being unwound
the prayers my friend had enscrolled in real time.

---

* *Yaar*: Hindi word for friend.

The throat of the rearview and sliding down it
the Street of Farewell's now unrolled in real time.

I heard the incessant dissolving of silk —
I felt my heart growing so old in real time.

Her heart must be ash where her body lies burned.
What hope lets your hands rake the cold in real time?

Now Friend, the Belovéd has stolen your words —
Read slowly: The plot will unfold in real time.

(for Daniel Hall)

On Hearing a Lover Not Seen
for Twenty Years Has
Attempted Suicide

I suspect it was over me.

Suicide Note*

I could not simplify myself.

Ghazal

Where should we go after the last frontiers,
where should the birds fly after the last sky?
—MAHMOUD DARWISH

In Jerusalem a dead phone's dialed by exiles.
You learn your strange fate: You were exiled by exiles.

One opens the heart to list unborn galaxies.
Don't shut that folder when Earth is filed by exiles.

Before Night passes over the wheat of Egypt,
let stones be leavened, the bread torn wild by exiles.

Crucified Mansoor* was alone with the Alone:
God's loneliness—Just His—compiled by exiles.

By the Hudson lies Kashmir, brought from Palestine—
It shawls the piano, Bach beguiled by exiles.

Tell me who's tonight the Physician of Sick Pearls?
Only you as you sit, Desert child, by exiles.

Match Majnoon** (he kneels to pray on a wine-stained rug)
or prayer will be nothing, distempered mild by exiles.

"Even things that are true can be proved." Even they?
Swear not by Art but, dear Oscar Wilde, by exiles.

Don't weep, we'll drown out the Call to Prayer, O Saqi—
I'll raise my glass before wine is defiled by exiles.

* Mansoor: Mansoor al-Hallaj, the great Muslim mystic martyr who was crucified in Baghdad for saying "I am the Truth."

** Majnoon: Literally, "possessed" or "mad" because he sacrificed everything for love.

Was — after the last sky — this the fashion of fire:
Autumn's mist pressed to ashes styled by exiles?

If my enemy's alone and his arms are empty,
give him my heart silk-wrapped like a child by exiles.

Will you, Belovéd Stranger, ever witness Shahid —
two destinies at last reconciled by exiles?

The Purse-Seiner *Atlantis*

Black Pacific. "Shahid, come here, quick." A ship,
giant lantern held in its own light, the dark
left untouched, a phantom-ship with birds, no, moths,

giant moths that cannot die. Which world has sent
it? And which awaits its cargo's circling light,
staggered halo made of wings? The dark is still,

fixed around that moving lamp which keeps the light
so encased it pours its milk into itself,
sailing past with moths that cannot put themselves

out. What keeps this light from pouring out as light?
Beautiful in white, she says, "I'll just be back."
She goes inside. I fill my glass till I see

everything and nothing stare back at me, fill
me with longing, the longing to long, to be
flame, and moth, and ash. What light now startles me?

Neighbor's window. *Turn it off, God, turn it off.*
When they do, a minute later, I am—what?
Ash completely, yet not ash, I see I am

what is left of light, what light leaves me, what light
always leaves of me. "Oh, Shahid" (from inside
her voice is light), "could you light the candles, please?"

"Come back out, the ship is close." Moths, one by one,
dive into the light, dive deep to catch the light,
then return to keep the halo. Ship, what ghost

keeps you moving north? Your light is pouring flames
down your sides, yet all the sea keeps dark. What waits
for you beyond—seas and continents erased

from every map? The halo thickens. Yet what
keeps the sky untouched, so dark? She comes outside.
"Do you like the wine? I bought it years ago."

"It is the best ever." When I next look out
("Nothing lasts, of course"), the ship has disappeared.
The dark completes itself. What light now strikes us?

"Look, the phosphorus." It streaks the shore, it shines
green, bottle green, necklace darkened round the shore
where we now are walking by Time's stray wreckage

(broken planks, black glass) while the waves, again,
repeat each rumor the sea, out there, denies—
chilled necklaces, lost continents, casks of wine.

(for Elena Karina Byrne)

Eleven Stars Over Andalusia

Poem by Mahmoud Darwish: Version by Agha Shahid Ali (with Ahmad Dallal)

1. On our last evening on this land

On our last evening on this land we chop our days
from our young trees, count the ribs we'll take with us
and the ribs we'll leave behind . . . On the last evening
we bid nothing farewell, nor find the time to end . . .
Everything remains as it is, it is the place that changes our dreams
and its visitors. Suddenly we're incapable of irony,
this land will now host atoms of dust . . . Here, on our last evening,
we look closely at the mountains besieging the clouds: a conquest . . .
    and a counter-conquest,
and an old time handing this new time the keys to our doors.
So enter our houses, conquerors, and drink the wine
of our mellifluous *Mouwashah*.* We are the night at midnight,
and no horseman will bring dawn from the sanctuary of the last Call
    to Prayer . . .
Our tea is green and hot; drink it. Our pistachios are fresh; eat
    them.
The beds are of green cedar, fall on them,
following this long siege, lie down on the feathers of our dreams.
The sheets are crisp, perfumes are ready by the door, and there are
    plenty of mirrors:
Enter them so we may exit completely. Soon we will search
in the margins of your history, in distant countries,
for what was once *our* history. And in the end we will ask ourselves:
Was Andalusia here or there? On the land . . . or in the poem?

---

  * *Mouwashah*: The characteristic form of Andalusian poetry, recited and sung.
Still performed throughout the Arab world.

2. How can I write above the clouds?

How can I write my people's testament above the clouds when they
abandon me as they do their coats at home, my people
who raze each fortress they build and pitch on its ruins
a tent, nostalgic for the beginning of palm trees? My people betray
    my people
in wars over salt. But Granada is made of gold,
of silken words woven with almonds, of silver tears
in the string of a lute. Granada is a law unto herself:
It befits her to be whatever she wants to be: nostalgia for
anything long past or which will pass. A swallow's wing brushes
a woman's breast, and she screams: "Granada is my body."
In the meadow someone loses a gazelle, and he screams, "Granada is
    my country."
And I come from there . . . So sing until from my ribs the
    goldfinches can build
a staircase to the nearer sky. Sing of the chivalry of those who
    ascend,
moon by moon, to their death in the Belovéd's alley. Sing the birds
    of the garden,
stone by stone. How I love you, you who have broken me,
string by string, on the road to her heated night. Sing how,
after you, the smell of coffee has no morning. Sing of my departure,
from the cooing of doves on your knees and from my soul nesting
in the mellifluous letters of your name. Granada is for singing, so
    sing!

3. There is a sky beyond the sky for me

There is a sky beyond the sky for my return, but
I am still burnishing the metal of this place, living in
an hour that foresees the unseen. I know that time
cannot twice be on my side, and I know that I will leave —
I'll emerge, with wings, from the banner I am, bird
that never alights on trees in the garden —
I will shed my skin and my language.
Some of my words of love will fall into
Lorca's poems; he'll live in my bedroom
and see what I have seen of the Bedouin moon. I'll emerge
from almond trees like cotton on sea foam. The stranger passed,
carrying seven hundred years of horses. The stranger passed
here to let the stranger pass there. In a while I'll emerge a stranger
from the wrinkles of my time, alien to Syria and to Andalusia.
This land is not my sky, yet this evening is mine.
The keys are mine, the minarets are mine, the lamps are mine,
and I am also mine. I am Adam of the two Edens, I who lost
	paradise twice.
So expel me slowly,
and kill me slowly,
under my olive tree,
along with Lorca . . .

4. I am one of the kings of the end

. . . And I am one of the kings of the end . . . I jump
off my horse in the last winter. I am the last gasp of an Arab.
I do not look for myrtle over the roofs of houses, nor do I
look around: No one should know me, no one should recognize me,
    no one who knew me
when I polished marble words to let my woman step
barefoot over dappled light. I do not look into the night, I mustn't
see a moon that once lit up all the secrets of Granada,
body by body. I do not look into the shadow, so as not to see
somebody carrying my name and running after me: Take your name
    away from me
and give me the silver of the white poplar. I do not look behind me,
    so I won't remember
I've passed over this land, there is no land in this land
since time broke around me, shard by shard.
I was not a lover believing that water is a mirror,
as I told my old friends, and no love can redeem me,
for I've accepted the "peace accord" and there is no longer a present
    left
to let me pass, tomorrow, close to yesterday. Castile will raise
its crown above God's minaret. I hear the rattling of keys
in the door of our golden history. Farewell to our history! Will I be
the one to close the last door of the sky, I, the last gasp of an Arab?

5. One day I will sit on the pavement

One day I will sit on the pavement . . . the pavement of the
    estranged.
I was no Narcissus; still I defend my image
in the mirrors. Haven't you been here once before, stranger?
Five hundred years have passed, but our breakup wasn't final,
and the messages between us never stopped. The wars
did not change the gardens of my Granada. One day I'll pass its
    moons
and brush my desire against a lemon tree . . . Embrace me and let
    me be reborn
from the scents of sun and river on your shoulders, from your feet
that scratch the evening until it weeps milk to accompany the poem's
    night . . .
I was not a passer-by in the words of singers . . . I was the words
of the singers, the reconciliation of Athens and Persia, an East
    embracing a West
embarked on one essence. Embrace me that I may be born again
from Damascene swords hanging in shops. Nothing remains of me
but my old shield and my horse's gilded saddle. Nothing remains of
    me
but manuscripts of Averroës, *The Collar of the Dove,** and translations.

. . .

---

* *The Collar of the Dove*: A celebrated treatise on love by Ibn Hazm of Cordoba.

On the pavement, in the Square of the Daisy,
I was counting the doves: one, two, thirty . . . and the girls
snatching the shadows of the young trees over the marble, leaving
    me
leaves yellow with age. Autumn passed me by, and I did not notice
the entire season had passed. Our history passed me on the
    pavement

. . .

and I did not notice.

6. Truth has two faces and the snow is black

Truth has two faces and the snow falls black on our city.
We can feel no despair beyond our despair,
and the end—firm in its step—marches to the wall,
marching on tiles that are wet with our tears.
Who will bring down our flags: we or they? And who
will recite the "peace accord," O king of dying?
Everything's prepared for us in advance; who will tear our names
from our identity: you or they? And who will instill in us
the speech of wanderings: "We were unable to break the siege;
let us then hand the keys to our paradise to the Minister of Peace,
    and be saved . . ."
Truth has two faces. To us the holy emblem was a sword
hanging over us. So what did you do to our fortress before this day?
You didn't fight, afraid of martyrdom. Your throne is your coffin.

Carry then the coffin to save the throne, O king of waiting,
this exodus will leave us only a handful of dust . . .
Who will bury our days after us: you . . . or they? And who
will raise their banners over our walls: you . . . or
a desperate knight? Who will hang their bells on our journey:
you . . . or a miserable guard? Everything is fixed for us:
why, then, this unending conclusion, O king of dying?

7. Who am I after the night of the estranged?

Who am I after the night of the estranged? I wake from my dream,
frightened of the obscure daylight on the marble of the house, of
the sun's darkness in the roses, of the water of my fountain;
frightened of milk on the lip of the fig, of my language;
frightened of wind that — frightened — combs a willow; frightened
of the clarity of petrified time, of a present no longer
a present; frightened, passing a world that is no longer
my world. Despair, be merciful. Death, be
a blessing on the stranger who sees the unseen more clearly than
a reality that is no longer real. I'll fall from a star
in the sky into a tent on the road to . . . where?
Where is the road to anything? I see the unseen more clearly than
a street that is no longer my street. Who am I after the night of the
      estranged?
Through others I once walked toward myself, and here I am,
losing that self, those others. My horse disappeared by the Atlantic,
and by the Mediterranean I bleed, stabbed with a spear.
Who am I after the night of the estranged? I cannot return to

my brothers under the palm tree of my old house, and I cannot
    descend to
the bottom of my abyss. You, the unseen! Love has no heart . . .
no heart in which I can dwell after the night of the estranged . . .

8. O water, be a string to my guitar

O water, be a string to my guitar. The conquerors arrived,
and the old conquerors left. It is difficult to remember my face
in the mirrors. Water, be my memory, let me see what I have lost.
Who am I after this exodus? I have a rock
with my name on it, on a hill from which I see what's long gone . . .
Seven hundred years escort me beyond the city wall . . .
In vain time turns to let me salvage my past from a moment
that gives birth to my exile . . . and others' . . .
To my guitar, O water, be a string. The conquerors arrived,
and the old conquerors left, heading southward, repairing their days
in the trashheap of change: I know who I was yesterday, but who
    will I be
in a tomorrow under Columbus's Atlantic banners? Be a string,
be a string to my guitar, O water! There is no *Misr** in Egypt,
no Fez** in Fez, and Syria draws away. There is no falcon in
my people's banner, no river east of the palm groves besieged
by the Mongols' fast horses. In which Andalusia do I end? Here
or there? I will know I've perished and that here I've left
the best part of me: my past. Nothing remains but my guitar.

   * Misr: "Urban life," but also "Egypt."
   ** Fez: Arabic *Fas*; also means "ax."

Then be to my guitar a string, O water. The old conquerors left,
the new conquerors arrived.

9. In the exodus I love you more

In the exodus I love you more. In a while
you will lock the city's gates. There is no heart for me in your hands,
    and no
road anywhere for my journey. In this demise I love you more.
After your breast, there is no milk for the pomegranate at our
    window.
Palm trees have become weightless,
the hills have become weightless, and streets in the dusk have
    become weightless;
the earth has become weightless as it bids farewell to its dust. Words
    have become weightless,
and stories have become weightless on the staircase of night. My
    heart alone is heavy,
so let it remain here, around your house,
barking, howling for a golden time.
It alone is my homeland. In the exodus I love you more,
I empty my soul of words: I love you more.
We depart. Butterflies lead our shadows. In exodus
we remember the lost buttons of our shirts, we forget
the crown of our days, we remember the apricot's sweat, we forget
the dance of horses on festival nights. In departure
we become only the birds' equals, merciful to our days, grateful for
    the least.

I am content to have the golden dagger that makes my murdered
    heart dance —
kill me then, slowly, so I may say: I love you more than
I had said before the exodus. I love you. Nothing hurts me,
neither air nor water . . . neither basil in your morning nor
iris in your evening, nothing hurts me after this departure.

10. I want from love only the beginning

I want from love only the beginning. Doves patch,
over the squares of my Granada, this day's shirt.
There is wine in our clay jars for the feast after us.
In the songs there are windows: enough for blossoms to explode.

I leave jasmine in the vase; I leave my young heart
in my mother's cupboard; I leave my dream, laughing, in water;
I leave the dawn in the honey of the figs; I leave my day and my
    yesterday
in the passage to the Square of the Orange where doves fly.

Did I really descend to your feet so speech could rise,
a white moon in the milk of your nights . . . pound the air
so I could see the Street of the Flute blue . . . pound the evening
so I could see how this marble between us suffers?

The windows are empty of the orchards of your shawl. In another
    time
I knew so much about you. I picked gardenias
from your ten fingers. In another time there were pearls for me
around your neck, and a name on a ring whose gem was darkness,
    shining.

I want from love only the beginning. Doves flew
in the last sky, they flew and flew in that sky.
There is still wine, after us, in the barrels and jars.
A little land will suffice for us to meet, a little land will be enough for
    peace.

11. Violins

Violins weep with gypsies going to Andalusia
Violins weep for Arabs leaving Andalusia

Violins weep for a time that does not return
Violins weep for a homeland that might return

Violins set fire to the woods of that deep deep darkness
Violins tear the horizon and smell my blood in the vein

Violins weep with gypsies going to Andalusia
Violins weep for Arabs leaving Andalusia

Violins are horses on a phantom string of moaning water
Violins are the ebb and flow of a field of wild lilacs

Violins are monsters touched by the nail of a woman now distant
Violins are an army, building and filling a tomb made of marble and
    *Nahawund**

Violins are the anarchy of hearts driven mad by the wind in a
    dancer's foot
Violins are flocks of birds fleeing a torn banner

Violins are complaints of silk creased in the lover's night
Violins are the distant sound of wine falling on a previous desire

Violins follow me everywhere in vengeance
Violins seek me out to kill me wherever they find me

Violins weep for Arabs leaving Andalusia
Violins weep with gypsies going to Andalusia

---

* *Nahawund*: One of the classical Arabic musical modes.

I Dream I Am at the Ghat of the Only World

A night of ghazals comes to an end. The singer
departs through her chosen mirror, her one diamond
cut on her countless necks. I, as ever, linger

till chandeliers dim to the blue of Samarkand
domes and I've again lost everyone. Which mirror
opened for JM's* descent to the skeletoned

dark? Will I know the waiting boat? The burnt water?
By which mirror Eqbal,** in his clear undertone,
still plots to end all human pain? When my mother

died, he had wept so far away in Pakistan . . .
In the growing dark, through my own mirror, steps lead me
to the boat. From which time do I know the oarsman?

*Don't you know me? You were a mere boy. For no money
I—I was a young man then—I always rowed you across
the Jhelum, of which this river's the ebony*

*ghost. Every wave I left untouched became glass
to reflect you. I left you untouched, I left you
perfect.*

    * JM: James Merrill. He speaks in capitals in the manner of voices from
the other world in his epic *The Changing Light at Sandover*.
      ** Eqbal: Eqbal Ahmad, celebrated political thinker and activist who died in 1999.

SO IT'S ANOTHER CHRONICLE OF LOSS . . .
AND LOVE. "Whose voice was that, fine out of" CLEAR DARK
    BLUE?
One who forsook you by dying, the way you forsook
me, and so many, by not dying. I've waited through —

what haven't I waited through? — but he's left a book
for you (I rowed him not long ago). It's right there.
I promised him I would keep it safe for you. Look

for it under your seat cushion. I find it. In fear
it will disappear I clutch it. Like a lost will,
a card falls out, its lowercase inked in austere

black: "Before his untimely death, James Merrill
requested" . . . I stop, for his heartstopping absence,
then finish: "Before his untimely death, James Merrill

requested that a copy of A SCATTERING OF SALTS,
now his last book, be sent to you with his compliments."

· · ·

The oarsman (SLAVE OF THE PROPHET . . . *That* was his
    name) . . .
The clock bell chimes, as it always did, in the Convent's
tower. Will he take me to the islands through the same

waters I know? The school day ends. The children's
laughter fills the waves. "Gula,* keeper of our decades"
(I glance, *a look askance*, through the table of contents),

"I know you now." *You've kept me waiting. In the shades
of islands they await letters their living have sent,
they whom (restless by the shrines) nothing persuades*

of their own death. But is she here, magnificent
still if this world's emptied of music? Will I find her?
With her I'd heard—on 78 rpm—*Peer Gynt* . . .

and Ghalib's grief in the voice of Begum Akhtar
(diamonded singer who, just moments ago, chose
her own mirror). What hadn't we heard together—

and said—by the river of which this is the ghost?
Upstream, after Zero Bridge . . . through a narrow canal
he rows. From somewhere it is "Ase's Death." We coast

along flood banks. Now the iron gates to the Dal.**
The music stops. "Will the authorities allow
the gates to open?" *The times are tyrannical*

* Gula the boatman: Gula is an affectionate name for Ghulam Mohommad
(Slave of Mohommad).

** Dal: Legendary lake, famous for its luxury houseboats and floating gardens.

and death is punctual. But as in boyhood, somehow
Gula has threatened with Hell or bribed with Heaven
some sleeping guard. We row past PARADISE ENOW,*

GULISTAN, FIRDAUSI, SHIRAZ, even
KHAYYAM. From each houseboat tourists from long ago
wave, longing for letters, frantic to tear open

envelopes. But they are stilled, always a tableau
when we approach. Gula leaves by their feet, in silence,
the letters I have brought, then returns to row

us, faster faster — *We should not keep your loved ones
waiting.* When I look back, nothing at all is heard
though I can see them furious in oblivion's

shade, crumpling postcards. *To whom will I row some word
of them when their wails have not even begun to die?*
An island of burnt chinars** appears, bulbuls† blurred —

without song — in their branches. What one could prophesy
in their shade is now lost to elegies in a shrine.
Gula always had candles for tombs, to occupy

* PARADISE ENOW, etc.: Houseboats with names (except for PARADISE ENOW)
of Persian poets.
  ** chinar: Giant plane tree.
  † bulbul: Persian songbird reminiscent of the nightingale.

their shades when he brought me here—always by design—
for by his secret cash in the back, once afloat,
he showed me, right here, jasmine sticks for the Divine.

. . .

But the trees have vanished when I step off the boat.
Instead there is a house, the one in Amherst, the one
where my mother fought death, by heart able to quote—

to the last—from the Urdu of Ghalib, from the Persian
of Hafiz. I keep ringing the bell. Eqbal Ahmad
opens the door, embraces me, "Where's the oarsman?

You should have asked him in." "There's only news of blood
out there in Kashmir. Whom will he ferry while
I'm here with you? I can't tell. But before the flood—

it's raining hard—he must let the dead reconcile
themselves to their shores." I run from window to window—
the boat is still moored. "Shahid, when you smile,

it seems your mother has returned to life. We all know
how you—you all—miss her. You all kept her alive
all those months, how you all fought death with her, although

love doesn't help anyone finally survive.
But she knew you would keep her alive, that you were
completely in love with her. Now *Khuda Hafiz.** I've

nothing more to say, for even here a voyager,
I always move in my heart between sad countries.
But let it not end" IT WON'T "this grief for your mother.

She is on the shrine-island where the Kashmiris,
from martyred voices, salve their every dirge, sublime
till the end." "What will she do when I'm on my knees

in the shrine? And Gula, where to now?" *We have time*
left for only one destination, so we must
bypass the magic I've told you of, island where I'm

always given a dream, sole letter one of the dead entrusts
to me to row safely to someone terribly missed,
someone among the living. Eqbal asked me just

today if his dream . . . "Yes, it was the catalyst
whereby I lost all fear of death, hearing him aslant,
'I am in a beautiful place, but to exist

here is so lonely.'" *Now he'll have peace, for he can't*
send any more dreams. "Tell him it's reached every shore,
that it lives in the world, on its own, resonant

* *Khuda Hafiz*: "God be with you" in Farsi.

with no change, that it is safe with us evermore,
that it is only with his dream that you could pave
your way through these waves to me. For in each wave your oar

hits I die, no longer untouched. In each I am slave,
Slave of the Prophet, to you. What else can be mine?
I do not forsake you. How long before the saint's grave?"

We are almost there. Here, take my candles, my jasmine.
Remember, our time will be brief here. We are hardly
here, waves have lost their ebony shine. Inside the shrine

Our time will be brief here
     I see desecration, God's tapestry
ripped, the faded chant of "There is no god but God
and Mohammed . . ." emptied of its eternity.

Only the wind—since when?—has lived here, in one awed
fright of boots, of soldiers. Now the cry of the gazelle—
it breaks the heart into the final episode.

Already it is night? Or light? Here one cannot tell.
She ties round my wrist (I'm on my knees) the saint's thread:
"May this always keep you safe from the flames of Hell."

. . .

With a night of ghazals, what else comes to an end?
If steps bring her back from the river, will Eqbal
also climb to the back of his glass with some legend

of freedom? We wait by his mirror in the hall.
On which unknown future—or past—does all depend?
Again the air awaits "Morning Mood" or a ghazal

to be what survives after sacrilege, to rend
the light—or dark—as chandeliers dim. I look out
the shrine's blood-stained panes to see curtains descend

on all sides of the boat. Still among the devout,
I cry, "Mother, will I lose you again, and in this,
the only world left? Won't the world, ashamed without

you, find its shrines bereft of any premise
of God?" She enters the boat. I run out in the rain.
"Will I wait here, alone, by this ebony abyss,

abandoned by you, alone?" WITH THE GREAT GOD PAIN
"Son, live long, I've died to wait for you all your life.
So you won't weep night and day for me, or the slain,

I will tighten this thread." "But this is the knife that"
NEVER FALLING KILLS?
                            Weep, for this is farewell,
To be rowed forever is the last afterlife

I cry out by the shrine door "I am no infidel
but on my knees on shore the believer in the rain—"
This is farewell I have rowed you this is farewell

"—believer Mother still on his knees in the rain
who knows that you even veiled are the one who employs
her touch like a lamp to show me again and again

to myself." AND THE LOVER COLDER AND WISER destroys
all hope . . . He is Death . . . His is the moving finger . . .
The boat enters fog . . . which thickens to clear . . . for one voice:

WEEPING? YOU MUST NOT. I ask, "Which world will bring her
back, or will he who wears his heart on his sleeve eaves-
drop always, in his inmost depths, on a cruel harbinger?"

SHAHID, HUSH. THIS IS ME, JAMES. THE LOVED ONE
    ALWAYS LEAVES.

CALL ME ISHMAEL
TONIGHT

The Ghazal

The ghazal can be traced back to seventh-century Arabia. In its canonical Persian (Farsi) form, arrived at in the eleventh century, it is composed of autonomous or semi-autonomous couplets that are united by a strict scheme of rhyme, refrain, and line length. The opening couplet sets up the scheme by having it in both lines, and then the scheme occurs only in the second line of every succeeding couplet—i.e., the first line (same length) of every succeeding couplet sets up a suspense, and the second line (same length but with the rhyme and refrain—the rhyme immediately preceding the refrain) delivers on that suspense by amplifying, dramatizing, imploding, exploding.

—Agha Shahid Ali

I Have Loved

I must go back briefly to a place I have loved
to tell you those you will efface I have loved.

For You

Did we run out of things or just a name for you?
Above us the sun doubles its acclaim for you.

Negative sun or negative shade pulled from the ground . . .
and the image brought in one ornate frame for you.

At my every word they cry, "Who the hell are you?"
What would you reply if they thus sent Fame to you?

What a noise the sentences make writing themselves—
Here's every word that we used as a flame for you.

I remember your wine in my springtime of sorrow.
Now the world lies broken. Is it the same for you?

Because in this dialect the eyes are crossed or quartz,
A STATUE A RAZOR A FACT I exclaim for you.

The birthplace of written language is bombed to nothing.
How neat, dear America, is this game for you?

The angel of history wears all expressions at once.
What will you do? Look, his wings are aflame for you.

On a visitor's card words are arranged in a row—
Who was I? Who am I? I've brought my claim. For you.

A pity I don't know if you're guilty of something!
I would—without your knowing—take the blame for you.

Still for many days the rain will continue to fall . . .
A voice will say, "I'm burning, God, in shame for You."

Something like smoke rises from the snuffed-out distance . . .
Whose house did that fire find which once came for you?

God's dropped the scales. Whose wings will cover me, Michael?
Don't pronounce the sentence Shahid overcame for you.

(for Michael Palmer)

Of It All

I say *This, after all, is the trick of it all*
when suddenly you say "Arabic of it all."

After Algebra there was Geometry—and then Calculus—
But I'd already failed the arithmetic of it all.

White men across the U.S. love their wives' curries—
I say *O No!* to the turmeric of it all.

"Suicide represents . . . a privileged moment. . . ."
Then what keeps you—and me—from being sick of it all?

The telephones work, but I'm still cut off from you.
We star in *America*, fast epic of it all.

What shapes galaxies and keeps them from flying apart?
There's that missing mass, the black magic of it all.

What makes yours the rarest edition is just this:
it's bound in human skin, final fabric of it all.

I'm smashed, fine Enemy, in your isolate mirror.
Why the diamond display then—in public—of it all?

Before the palaver ends, hear the sparrows' songs,
the quick quick quick, O the quick of it all.

For the suicidally beautiful, autumn now starts.
Their fathers' heroes, boys gallop, kick off it all.

The sudden storm swept its ice across the great plains.
How did you find me, then, in the thick of it all?

Across the world one aches for New York, but to long
for New York in New York's most tragic of it all.

For Shahid too the night went "quickly as it came"—
After that, old friend, came the music of it all.

(for Anthony Lacavaro)

Of Fire

In a mansion once of love I lit a chandelier of fire . . .
I stood on a stair of water; I stood on a stair of fire.

When, to a new ghost, I recited, "Is That What You Are,"
at the windows in the knives he combed his hair of fire.

You have remained with me even in the missing of you.
Could a financier then ask me for a new share of fire?

I keep losing this letter to the gods of abandon.
Won't you tell me how you found it—in what hemisphere of fire?

Someone stirs, after decades, in a glass mountain's ruins.
Is Death a cry from an age that was a frozen year of fire?

I have brought my life here where it must have been once,
my wings, still hope and grief, but singed by a courtier of fire.

When the Husband of Water touched his Concubine of Snow,
he hardened to melt in their private affair of fire.

Don't lose me in the crowds of this world's cities,
or the Enemy may steal from me what gods revere of fire.

The way we move into a dream we won't ever remember,
statues will now move into wars for a career of fire.

What lights up the buildings? My being turned away! O, the injustice
as I step through a hoop of tears, all I can bare of fire.

Soldier: "The enemy can see you and that's how you die."
On the world's roof, breathless, he defends a glacier of fire.

I have come down to my boat to wish myself *Bon Voyage*.
If that's the true sound of brevity, what will reappear of fire?

A designer of horizons, I've come knocking at your door.
Buy my sunsets, please, for the Pacific's interior of fire.

I could not improve my skill to get ahead of storms though
I too enrolled in Doomsday to be a courier of fire.

"on the last day of one September" "one William was born"
Native of Water, Shahid's brought the Kashmir of fire.

(for W. S. Merwin)

Things

Blood, Hook & Eye: Certainly here lay true true things
for *Our Master Plan* —by the plough —among blue things.

About the death penalty —as you held back a tear —
even the children cried out that they foreknew things.

"The two houses in which I was raised were torn down."
Summers raced to autumnal lands to bedew things.

"I could not find you and feared I'd never find you . . ."
Then out of the blue you called me. You value —things?

He "can't get called / on . . . or taken to the cleaners"
though it's time for Anonymous to shampoo things.

It snowed. Then I had no home. Way way back beyond
with the exact meaning of faith I'll argue things.

Black Death inhabits his field with fascinating pain
and burns down the accrued Muslim-Christian-Jew things.

Your country also had no post office until now?
"But now no one's left to write to there" —Ah! —to do things.

I, from the upper berth, slip "down into her dream."
Choo-choo "Goes the train towards" some déjà-vu things.

I save threadbare tapestries, stained silks, ripped cashmeres.
They say, *Now's the time to buy, to be into things*.

Has a narrow bridge in a flat valley at last
led me to Paradox proper to see through things?

Silence is the keeper of the keys to secrets.
"I can't talk to my wife / but I can to you" — *THINGS!*

He goes through his motions like a ghost while I am
doomed to watch him forsake me to interview things.

Shahid, I'm *Oak*, then *Angel of rains and rivers*.
Ah well, *Dara* also, like your name, means two things.

(for Dara Wier)

Shines

Suspended in the garden, Time, bit by bit, shines—
As "you lean over this page, / late and alone, it shines."

I've rushed to the country in which pain is asleep.
Its capital, for your unannounced visit, shines.

O Wailing Wall O Holy Sepulchre O Far Mosque
The Tunnel echoes stones, but still no exit shines.

Reasons for moving? Sleeping with one eye open!
But *Darker's* first edition at the exhibit shines.

Dying to be cast in saffron plaster—the Brahmin's!—
a soul (they mean the Untouchable's?) in transit shines?

Water drops on the burner its sizzling red pearls.
Moonlight, nude on the apricots of Gilgit, shines.

"The mirror / is in the living room. / You are there."
The cold place one body took—which I'll inhabit—shines.

WHAT THE THUNDER SAID Shantih Shantih Shantih
The peace that passeth understanding in Sanskrit shines.

Have you invented an ending that comes out right?
Judgment Day is already here, and no Writ shines.

Mark how Shahid returns your very words to you—
It's when the heart, still unbriefed, but briefly lit, shines.

(for Mark Strand)

My Word

I am lying even now—I give you my word.
Kind of a picnic, an occupied shoe. My word!

My telegram arrives, no one's there to read it—
not even he who on tombs will bedew my word.

Danger invites rescue, we have a good thing going.
So let's break everything, please rescue my word.

The ghost said nothing that added to our knowledge.
Upon the candle—which lit itself—who blew my word?

I'm at home, betrothed to blue, with her refracted light.
The light is home, this blue is blue all through my word.

Hard to say who's winning. Nobody is winning.
Kansas City! Oriental art! Big Zoo! My word!

I took the shortest route through Belief's sad country
when archangels, on the Word's command, slew my word.

This erasure tilts words toward memory or tilts
against your word—at the tiny hour of two—my word.

Forgive me, please, could we be alone forever?
I have never been alone; I'll live to rue my word.

Our silence, Beloved Enemy, is not beyond
whatever love has done to your word, to my word.

Now don't put on, please, that face, just wait for me here.
I stand no one up. See you in a few. My word.

Will the barbarians bring again their invisible language?
They were the solution, they foreknew my word.

Yours too, Shahid, will be a radical departure.
You'll go out of yourself and then into my word.

(for James Tate)

From The Start

The Belovéd will leave you behind from the start.
Light is difficult: one must be blind from the start.

You begin to feel better when the clocks are set back?
Child of northern darkness — so defined from the start.

Between two snow-heavy boughs, perhaps a bright star?
Or in one sparkling many stars combined from the start?

Ontological episode? God doesn't care.
"That is why he exists," you divined from the start.

Solomon's throne was a toy, his Judgment mere talk —
Only our sins must be enshrined from the start.

Poet, tell me again how the white heron rises.
For the spirit, they say, is confined from the start.

To *What is mind?* we swiftly answer *O, no matter!*
Those who know matter never mind from the start.

Will the middle class give up its white devotions?
Feed their infants cayenne and tamarind from the start.

I am mere dust. The desert hides itself in me.
Against me the ocean has reclined from the start.

Who but Satan can know God's sorrow in Heaven?
God longs for the lover He undermined from the start.

"But I / am here in this real life / that I was given. . . ."
To what else should we be resigned from the start?

You have dwelt at the root of a scream forever—
The Forever Shahid's countersigned from the start.

(for Hayden Carruth)

Angels

The pure pain with which he recognizes angels
has left him without cures among the dreamless angels.

The dawn looked over its shoulder to ask the naked night
for the new fashions in which it could dress angels.

Is it that I've been searching in the wrong places for you?
That your address is still Los Angeles, Angels?

The air is my vinegar, I, its perfect preserve—
Watch how I'm envied by Heaven's meticulous angels.

In Inferno the walls mirror brocades and silks.
Satan's legions—though fallen—are, nonetheless, angels.

"Let there be Light," He said. "And the music of the spheres."
To what tune does one set *The Satanic Verses*, Angels?

I won't lift, off the air, any wingprints, O God—
Hire raw detectives to track down the mutinous angels.

All day we call it wisdom but then again at night
it's only pain as it comes from the darkness, Angels!

Why is God so frightened of my crazy devotion to Him?
Does he think that, like Satan, I too will finesse angels?

Do they dye their wings after Forever, tinting their haloes,
aging zero without Time, those androgynous angels?

You play innocence so well, with such precision, Shahid:
You could seduce God Himself, and fuck the sexless angels.

Of Water

But first the screened mirror, all I knew of water!
Imagine "the thirstquenching virtue of water."

Who "kept on building castles" "Upon a certain rock"
"Glacial warden over 'dreams come true'" of water?

Of course, I saw Chile in my rearview mirror,
its disappeared under a curfew of water.

Hagar, in shards, reflects her shattered Ishmael.
Call her the desert Muslim—or Jew—of water.*

God, Wordless, beheld the pulled rain but missed the held sun . . .
The Rainbow—that Arrow!—Satan's coup of water.

Don't beckon me, Love, to the island of your words—
You yourself reached it, erasing my view of water.

Her star-cold palanquin goes with the caravan.
Majnoon, now she'll be news—out of the blue—of water.

When the Beast takes off his mask, Love, let it be you
sweetening Tomorrow Doom's taboo of water.

No need to stop the ears to the Sirens' rhetoric;
just mock their rock-theme, you skeleton crew of water.

* When Hagar and Ishmael were left in the desert, God answered Hagar's plea
for water for the infant Ishmael with the Zumzum spring in Mecca.

Are your streets, Abraham, washed of "the Sons of Stones"?
Sand was all Ishmael once drew of water.

I have signed, O my enemy, your death-warrant.
I won't know in time I am like you of water.

For God's sake don't unveil the Black Stone of K'aaba.
What if Faith too's let love bead a dew of water?

I have even become tears to live in your eyes.
If you weep, Stark Lover, for my breakthrough of water?

Shahid's junk mail has surfaced in a dead-letter office.
He's deluxed in the leather *Who's Who of Water*.

As Ever

(after Ahmad Faraz)

So I'll regret it. But lead my heart to pain.
Return, if it is just to leave me again.

"Till death do us part." Come for their sense of *us* . . .
For Belief's sake, let appearances remain.

Let YOU, at Elysian Fields, step off the streetcar—
so my sense of wonder's made utterly plain.

Not for mine but for the world's sake come back.
They ask why you left? To whom all must I explain?

I laughed when they said our time was running out—
I stirred the leaves in the tea I'd brewed to drain.

Break your pride, be the Consoler for once—
Bring roses, let my love-illusion remain.

An era's passed since the luxury of tears—
Make me weep, Consoler, let blood know its rain.

From New York to Andalusia I searched for you—
Lorca, dazzled on your lips, is all of Spain.

"Time, like Love, wears a mask in this story."
And Love? My blind spot. Piercing me to the brain.

Oh, that my head were waters, mine eyes a fountain
so that I might weep day and night for the slain.

Shouting your name till the last car had disappeared,
how I ran on the platform after your train.

To find her, 'round phantom-wrists I glue bangles —
What worlds she did not break when she left my lane!

Still beguiled with hopes of you, the heart is lit.
To put out this last candle, come, it burns in vain.

Land

Swear by the olive in the God-kissed land—
There is no sugar in the promised land.

Why must the bars turn neon now when, Love,
I'm already drunk in your capitalist land?

If home is found on both sides of the globe,
home is of course here—and always a missed land.

The hour's come to redeem the pledge (not wholly?)
in Fate's "Long years ago we made a tryst" land.

Clearly, these men were here only to destroy,
a mosque now the dust of a prejudiced land.

Will the Doomsayers die, bitten with envy,
when springtime returns to our dismissed land?

The prisons fill with the cries of children.
Then how do you subsist, how do you persist, Land?

"Is my love nothing for I've borne no children?"
I'm with you, Sappho, in that anarchist land.

A hurricane is born when the wings flutter . . .
Where will the butterfly, on my wrist, land?

You made me wait for one who wasn't even there
though summer had finished in that tourist land.

Do the blind hold temples close to their eyes
when we steal their gods for our atheist land?

Abandoned bride, Night throws down her jewels
so Rome — on our descent — is an amethyst land.

At the moment the heart turns terrorist,
are Shahid's arms broken, O Promised Land?

(for Christopher Merrill)

Not All, Only A Few Return

(after Ghalib)

Just a few return from dust, disguised as roses.
What hopes the earth forever covers, what faces?

I too could recall moonlit roofs, those nights of wine —
But Time has shelved them now in Memory's dimmed places.

She has left forever, let blood flow from my eyes
till my eyes are lamps lit for love's darkest places.

All is his — Sleep, Peace, Night — when on his arm your hair
shines to make him the god whom nothing effaces.

With wine, the palm's lines, believe me, rush to Life's stream —
Look, here's my hand, and here the red glass it raises.

See me! Beaten by sorrow, man is numbed to pain.
Grief has become the pain only pain erases.

World, should Ghalib keep weeping you will see a flood
drown your terraced cities, your marble palaces.

Water

When pilgrims brought back no bottles of Samarkand water,
everyone filled our samovars with almond water.

There was only a tea of the second water
we remembered home samovars with cinnamoned water.

As soon as springtime came in every house
we drank tea steeped in cardamom and almond water.

The floods left little of our land to us
but how grateful we were for the unsunned water.

A terrible time is coming *après vous après vous*
What fire will you find to refund water?

At the temple and the mosque the rose petals
lay all night perfuming the stunned water.

This may surprise you but after the forty days
the sunshine left us helpless with stunned water.

It was a dark time and everywhere the soldiers
had made sure we were thirsty for their garrisoned water.

So if this is indeed a matter of nature then the sky
was the flesh and its reflection was skeletoned water

What did your ancestor bring from Samarkand? Water?
In our samovars it becomes cardamom and almond water.

Of Snow

Husband of Water, where is your Concubine of Snow?
Has she laced your flooded desert with a wine of snow?

What a desert we met in—the foliage was lush!—
a cactus was dipped into every moonshine of snow.

One song is so solitaire in our ring of mountains,
its echo climbs to cut itself at each line of snow.

The sky beyond its means is always besides itself
till (by the plane) each peak rises, a shrine of snow.

Snowmen, inexplicably, have gathered in the Sahara
to melt and melt and melt for a Palestine of snow.

Kali turned to ice one winter, her veins transparent—
On her lips blood froze. A ruby wine of snow!

If Lorca were alive he would again come to New York,
bringing back to my life that one Valentine of snow.

Do you need to make angels, really, who then vanish
or are angels all you can undermine of snow?

I who believe in prayer but could never in God
place roses at your grave with nothing to divine of snow.

When he drinks in winter, Shahid kisses his enemies.
For Peace, then, let bars open at the first sign of snow.

Air

Drink this rain-dark rum of air
column of breath column of air.

About Me

(after some lines of Wisława Szymborska)

I'm too close, too close for him to dream about me,
for he is held (he is *al-Mustalim**) about me.

Now the grace to disappear from astonished eyes!
Note how I possess this—love's last!—theme about me.

Not so, my lord. "Seems," madam? Nay, it is. O God!
I am too much in the sun. I know not "seems" about me.

On the head of each pin dance the fallen angels.
If only they would needle the Supreme about me!

I pull my arm out from under his sleeping head,
limited to my own form, my scream about me.

My ears catch the rustling of last wills torn to pieces—
The dead so poor, infatuated, teem about me.

Now Christ will never die so readily for you,
left nailed with His wounds' sorry regime about me.

A house is on fire without my calling for help.
Like fangs in the dark, windowpanes gleam about me.

Elusively gay but not quite presently straight,
one is stone in his own forest stream about me.

---

* *al-Mustalim*: "The enraptured" in Arabic.

On Doomsday God asked the Pure, "Why didn't you sin?
Didn't you trust the best (*ar-Rahim**) about Me?"

I read letters of the dead and am a helpless god,
their bad taste, their electrical steam about me.

Father of Clay, this is Shahid; I am become flesh—
No spirit dusts or will itself redeem about me.

* *ar-Rahim*: "The Merciful"—one of God's ninety-nine names in Arabic. The traditional
Muslim prayer begins: "Begin in the Name of God, the Beneficent, the Merciful."

In Marble

Because there's no thyme or fenugreek in marble,
they say, "Let's go and play hide-and-seek in marble."

There on the tower (our life, our life, our life) —
watch the gull open and shut its beak in marble.

On her temple's black walls, Kali prints her tiger's
gold-red stripes till all's as if batik in marble.

Go where I will? Where will I go? Who hears my song
now that justice is radical chic in marble.

My lover went to Chisti's mother-of-pearl tomb
and almost found, calligraphed, my shriek in marble.

To be reduced to God's tears, from Heaven to Hell,
angels wail, and that too cheek-to-cheek in marble.

A penniless voyeur, I go downtown to see
Rodin's lovers—in one gift shop—peak in marble.

A hand broke. It was in plaster. I took it in mine.
He who was a god is now so bleak in marble.

Of course, I'll say something about the Taj Mahal
silvering in the moonlight all week in marble.

The sky, beyond itself, was beside itself when
above the clouds it saw mountains peak in marble.

From whose lips will a remembered god breathe at last?
If I am left mute, let someone else speak in marble.

Farewell, you museum-people, now leave me to face
my oracle spoken by an antique in marble.

Apollo (for weary way-worn wandering Shahid)
is yet another heartbreaking Greek in marble.

Bones

(after Hart Crane)

"I, too, was liege / To rainbows currying" pulsant bones.
The "sun took step of" Brooklyn Bridge's resonant bones.

From Far Rockaway to Golden Gate I saw blood
washed up on streets against God's irrelevant bones.

If the soul were a body, what would it insist on?
On smooth skin? On stubborn flesh? Or on elegant bones?

"The window goes blond slowly." And I beside you
am stripped and stripped and stripped to luxuriant bones.

So Elizabeth had two hundred Catholics burned
(Bloody Mary had loved the smoke of Protestant bones).

In the hair of Pocahontas a forest shudders.
Inventions cobblestone her extravagant bones.

They refuse to burn when we set fire to the flesh —
those flowers float down the Ganges as adamant bones.

"Footprints on the Glacier" are the snowman's — or mine?
Whosoever, they're found under some hesitant bones.

Someone once told us he had lost his pity for
(he did not qualify with "ignorant" or "tolerant") bones.

Migrating from me to me to me the soul asks
a bit seriously: What is our covenant, Bones?

Mustard oil, when heated, breaks out in veins which then
cayenne the sacrificed goat's most compliant bones.

The troops left our haven hanging in the night and said
the child's skeleton was made of militant bones.

And so it was Shahid entered the broken world
when everyone had bypassed the heart's expectant bones.

In

God to aggrandise, God to glorify
—GERARD MANLEY HOPKINS

Now "God to aggrandise, God to glorify" in
the candle that "clear burns"—glare I can't come by in.

What else for night-travel? The extra pair of socks?
Besides the tin of tea, pack the anti-fly in.

If you don't succeed at first, do certainly give up—
I too shut off those who say *Just keep tryin'!*

Galloping flood, hooves iron by the river's edge—
Heart, this beating night, how will you rein the sky in?

Thank you for the parchment and the voice of the sea.
A drowned god used the shell to send his reply in.

When the last leaves were birds, stuck wingless to branches,
the wind glass-stormed the season you'd left me to cry in.

Flood the market, O Blood, so the liver is restored,
again emotion's sea, the heart's forsaken tie-in.

By the Enemy, after battle, I place flowers
and the swords he'd heard the angels' lullaby in.

When even God is dead, what is left but prayer?
And this wilderness, the mirrors I multiply in?

When you missed its "feet and fur," JM, I too mourned
the caterpillar spring had sent the butterfly in.

Doomsday is over, Eden stretched vast before me —
I see the rooms, all the rooms, I am to die in.

Ere he never returns, he whose footsteps are dying,
Shahid, run out weeping, bring that passer-by in.

Beyond English

No language is old — or young — beyond English.
So what of a common tongue beyond English?

I know some words for war, all of them sharp,
but the sharpest one is *jung* — beyond English!

If you wish to know of a king who loved his slave,
you must learn legends, often-sung, beyond English.

Baghdad is sacked and its citizens must watch
prisoners (now in miniatures) hung beyond English.

Go all the way through *jungle* from *aleph* to *zenith*
to see English, like monkeys, swung beyond English.

So never send to know for whom the bell tolled,
for across the earth it has rung beyond English.

If you want your drugs legal you must leave the States,
not just for hashish but one — *bhung* — beyond English.

Heartbroken, I tottered out "into windless snow,"
snowflakes on my lips, silence stung beyond English.

When the phrase, "The Mother of all Battles," caught on,
the surprise was indeed not sprung beyond English.

Could a soul crawl away at last unshriveled which
to its "own fusing senses" had clung beyond English?

If someone asks where Shahid has disappeared,
he's waging a war (no, *jung*) beyond English.

(for Lawrence Needham)

Of Light

At dawn you leave. The river wears its skin of light.
And I trace love's loss to the origin of light.

"I swallow down the goodbyes I won't get to use."
At grief's speed she waves from a palanquin of light.

My book's been burned? Send me the ashes, so I can say:
I've been sent the phoenix in a coffin of light.

From History tears learn a slanted understanding
of the human face torn by blood's bulletin of light.

It was a temporal thought. Well, it has vanished.
Will Prometheus commit the mortal sin of light?

She said, "My name is icicles coming down from it . . ."
Did I leave it, somewhere, in a margin of light?

When I go off alone, as if listening for God,
there's absolutely nothing I can win of light.

Now everything's left to the imagination —
a djinn has deprived even Aladdin of light.

We'll see Manhattan, a bride in diamonds, one day
abashed to remind her sweet man, Brooklyn, of light.

"A cheekbone, / A curved piece of brow, / A pale eyelid . . ."
And the dark eye I make out with all within of light.

Stranger, when the river leans toward the emptiness,
abandon, for my darkness, the thick and thin of light.

"On these beaches / the sea throws itself down, in flames"
as we bring back, at sunset, the incarnadine of light.

Again on the point of giving away my heart,
Life is stalked by Fog, that blond assassin of light.

One day the streets all over the world will be empty;
from every tomb I'll learn all we imagine of light.

Galway, somehow with you in Freedom, New Hampshire,
Shahid won't let Death make of Love a ruin of light.

(for Galway Kinnell)

Stars

When through night's veil they continue to seep, stars
in infant galaxies begin to weep stars.

After the eclipse, there were no cheap stars
How can you be so cheap, stars?

How grateful I am you stay awake with me
till by dawn, like you, I'm ready to sleep, stars!

If God sows sunset embers in you, Shahid,
all night, because of you, the world will reap stars.

For Time

You who searched the world for a brave rhyme for time
got real lucky with a Guggenheim for time.

At the shrine I'll offer not roses but clocks.
When I return, I will have no time for time.

After the first death, there's only the first, which
with each death is now your paradigm for time.

All summer the news from the lost peaks said that
soldiers had died simply in a climb for time.

From new springtimes gather your loot of blossoms.
Let Kashmir arrest you for a crime for time.

Must we always cook with heartless substitutes?
Caraway for cumin *and* cloves? And lime for thyme?

When the blade became secretary to steel,
the knife's sanctuary was made sublime for time.

You never belonged even to yourself though
as you abandoned me your cry was *I'm for time*.

What a wonderful party! It is the Sabbath!
And everyone's cry is "Le Chaim." For time?

I really need a drink to be able to drink!
That clink — cracking ice — crystals my chime for time.

The Country of the Blind has ordered mirrors.
Its one-eyed king's vision is now prime for time.

The gravestones are filled with poetry or pathos?
Well, you knew the war was a pantomime for time.

Who amputates clock-hands to make you, Shahid,
await the god not there with all the time for time?

God

Of all things He's the King Allah King God.
Then why this fear of idolizing God?

Outgunned Chechens hold off Russian tanks—
They have a prayer. Are you listening, God?

I begged for prayers to the Surgeon's answer,
my heart alone against terrorizing God.

Masked, I hold him enthralled who's harmed me most—
I will hurt him as he's been hurting God.

So what make you of cosmic background noise?
Well, there's the Yoni (*My!*) and the Ling (*God!*).

A butterfly's wings flutter in the rain.
In which storm looms the fabricating God?

I believe in prayer and the need to believe—
even the great Nothing signifying God.

Of Fidelity I've made such high style
that, jealous of my perfect devotion,
even the angels come down from Heaven
and beg—beg—me to stop worshipping God.

How come you simply do not age, Shahid?
Well, I wish everyone well, including God.

Forever

Even Death won't hide the poor fugitive forever;
on Doomsday he will learn he must live forever.

Is that nectar the cry of the desert prophets?
See angels pour the Word through a sieve forever.

On the gibbet Hallaj cried *I Am the Truth*.
In this universe one dies a plaintive forever.

When parents fall in love with those blond assassins,
their children sign up for Western Civ forever.

With a brief note he quit the Dead Letter Office —
O World, they've lost Bartleby's missive forever.

Am I some Sinai, Moses, for lightning to char?
See me solarized, in negative forever.

In the heart's wild space lies the space of wilderness.
What won't one lose, what home one won't give forever!

A perfect stranger, he greeted herself in joy —
Not to be Tom, how lovely — she said — *I'm Viv forever!*

Jamshed, inventor of wine, saw the world in his cup.
Drink, cried his courtiers, *for he won't live forever.*

He lives by his wits, wears blue all day, stars all night.
Who would have guessed God would be a spiv forever?

Will the Enemy smile as I pass him on the street?
I'm still searching for someone to forgive forever.

As landscapes rise like smoke from their eyes, the blind hear
God swear by the fig and the olive forever.

The Hangman washes his hands, puts his son to sleep.
But for whom, come dawn, he's decisive forever?

Alone in His Cave — His Dance done — He's smeared with ash.
The Ganges flows from the head of Shiv forever.

You've forgiven everyone, Shahid, even God —
Then how could someone like you not live forever?

(for Donald Revell)

After You

We are left mute and so much is left unnamed after you—
No one is left in this world to be blamed after you.

Someone has disappeared after christening Bertha—
Shahid, will a hurricane ever be named after you?

Now from Miami to Boston Bertha is breaking her bones—
I find her in the parking lot. She says, "I'm blamed after you."

The Deluge would happen—it was claimed—after you
But the world did go on, unashamed, after you.

ANDREW BERTHA CHARLES DAVID ELLA FLOYD
    GEORGE
    but S comes so late in the alphabet that although
SHAHID DEVASTATES FLORIDA is your dream headline,
    no hurricane will ever be named after you.

In Arabic

(with revisions of some couplets of "Arabic")

A language of loss? I have some business in Arabic.
Love letters: calligraphy pitiless in Arabic.

At an exhibit of miniatures, what Kashmiri hairs!
Each paisley inked into a golden tress in Arabic.

This much fuss about a language I don't know? So one day
perfume from a dress may let you digress in Arabic.

A "Guide for the Perplexed" was written—believe me—
by Cordoba's Jew—Maimonides—in Arabic.

Majnoon, by stopped caravans, rips his collars, cries "Laila!"
Pain translated is O! much more—not less—in Arabic.

Writes Shammas: Memory, no longer confused, now is a homeland—
his two languages a Hebrew caress in Arabic.

When Lorca died, they left the balconies open and saw:
On the sea his *qasidas* stitched seamless in Arabic.

In the Veiled One's harem, an adultress hanged by eunuchs—
So the rank mirrors revealed to Borges in Arabic.

Ah, bisexual Heaven: wide-eyed houris and immortal youths!
To your each desire they say *Yes! O Yes!* in Arabic.

For that excess of sibilance, the last Apocalypse,
so pressing those three forms of S in Arabic.

I too, O Amichai, saw everything, just like you did—
In Death. In Hebrew. And (please let me stress) in Arabic.

They ask me to tell them what *Shahid* means: Listen, listen:
It means "The Belovéd" in Persian, "witness" in Arabic.

Tonight

Pale hands I loved beside the Shalimar
—LAURENCE HOPE

Where are you now? Who lies beneath your spell tonight?
Whom else from rapture's road will you expel tonight?

Those "Fabrics of Cashmere—" "to make Me beautiful—"
"Trinket"—to gem—"Me to adorn—How tell"—tonight?

I beg for haven: Prisons, let open your gates—
A refugee from Belief seeks a cell tonight.

God's vintage loneliness has turned to vinegar—
All the archangels—their wings frozen—fell tonight.

Lord, cried out the idols, *Don't let us be broken;*
Only we can convert the infidel tonight.

Mughul ceilings, let your mirrored convexities
multiply me at once under your spell tonight.

He's freed some fire from ice in pity for Heaven.
He's left open—for God—the doors of Hell tonight.

In the heart's veined temple, all statues have been smashed.
No priest in saffron's left to toll its knell tonight.

God, limit these punishments, there's still Judgment Day—
I'm a mere sinner, I'm no infidel tonight.

Executioners near the woman at the window.
Damn you, Elijah, I'll bless Jezebel tonight.

The hunt is over, and I hear the Call to Prayer
fade into that of the wounded gazelle tonight.

My rivals for your love—you've invited them all?
This is mere insult, this is no farewell tonight.

And I, Shahid, only am escaped to tell thee—
God sobs in my arms. Call me Ishmael tonight.

Existed

If you leave who will prove that my cry existed?
Tell me what was I like before I existed.

THE COUNTRY WITHOUT A POST OFFICE

The Blessèd Word

The poem, throughout, alludes to W. S. Merwin's translation of Osip Mandelstam's poem.

    Srinagar: The capital of Kashmir.

    Id-uz-Zuha: One of Islam's most sacred days. To establish centrality for Ishmael (Father of the Arab nation), Muslims say it was he—not Isaac—whom God had asked Abraham to sacrifice. The day is marked by festivity and the sacrifice of lambs and goats.

    Habba Khatun: I am indebted to M. Mujeeb's *Indian Muslims* (George Allen & Unwin) for the historical details and for some of my phrasing.

Farewell

This poem at one—but only one—level is a plaintive love letter from a Kashmiri Muslim to a Kashmiri Pandit (the indigenous Hindus of Kashmir are called Pandits).

Saffron: The world's best saffron is believed to be grown in Kashmir and Iran (it takes the stigmata of seventy-five thousand flowers to make one pound of saffron). A paste made from it is used in various Hindu rituals. The *color* saffron is associated with Hindu traditions, green with Muslim culture.

I See Kashmir from New Delhi at Midnight

Shah Hamdan (Sayyid 'Ali Hamadani): One often refers to his shrine in Srinagar simply by his name. A Sufi saint, he paid three visits to Kashmir (1372, 1379, and 1383), and he was in effect responsible for the peaceful conversion of the Kashmiris to Islam. On his third visit he was accompanied by seven hundred scholars and clerics who estalished Sufi centers throughout Kashmir.

Green thread: It is customary for both Muslims and Hindus to go to Sufi shrines and make a wish there by tying a thread. Should the wish come true, one must return to untie it.

I Dream I Am the Only Passenger on Flight 423 to Srinagar,

Begum Akhtar: One of the Indian subcontinent's greatest singers and certainly the greatest ghazal singer of all time. She died in 1974.

Lal Ded: Kashmiri mystic poet (1320?–1391?) whose verses are on almost every Kashmiri's lips. One of the many apocryphal legends associated with her has been recounted thus: "While wandering naked she spotted Hamadani [see the note for Shah Hamdan] and intuited his holiness. She cried out, 'I have seen a man!' and ran into a baker's shop, where she jumped into a blazing oven and was immediately consumed by the flames. When the saint came into the shop looking for her, she suddenly emerged from the oven dressed in an aura of the brilliant green of Paradise" (Daniel Halpern, ed. *Holy Fire*, HarperPerennial, p. 45).

Sheikh Noor-ud-Din (1377?–1438?): Patron saint of Kashmir who modernized the Kashmiri language. The destruction by fire of his shrine at Chrar-e-Sharif on 11 May 1995 was front-page news all over the world. John F. Burns reported in the *New York Times* (14 May 1995): "Despite Indian Army denials, the people who gathered to vent their fury insisted that it had been Indian troops, not Muslim militants besieged in the town, who set the fire—actually, two fires—that ran through the wondrous, toytown array of mostly wooden homes and bazaars and mosques that clung for centuries to the hillsides here, defying endless winters of bitter cold and summers of searing heat."

"On its pyre / the phoenix is dear to destiny": This is a free translation of a line of Sheikh Noor-ud-Din's, whose verses—marked by Sufi grace and wisdom—are also known to almost every Kashmiri.

A Fate's Brief Memoir

This poem is spoken by Clotho, whom I imagine to be the oldest of the three Fates. Among her conscious allusions are to Shakespeare, T. S. Eliot, George Trakl, Apollinaire, W. H. Auden, and Thomas Mann.

Norns: Also three sisters like the Greek Fates, they are the Fates of Scandinavian mythology.

"Farewell—and if thou livest or diest!": The first sentence of the last paragraph of Thomas Mann's *The Magic Mountain*.

ROOMS ARE NEVER FINISHED

Lenox Hill

"War's annals will fade into night / Ere their story die" is a direct quotation from Thomas Hardy's poem, "In Time of 'The Breaking of Nations.'"

Karbala: A History of the "House of Sorrow"

Most of this information—and some of the phrasing—is from Will Durant, *The Age of Faith*; Sayyid Muhammad Husayn Tabatabai, *Shi'a*; David Pinault, *The Shiites*; Heinz Halm, *Shi'a Islam: From Religion to Revolution*; and S. Husain M. Jafri, *Origins and Early Development of Shi'a Islam*. Except for a few details, the basic information is the same in all histories of Karbala.

To establish primacy for Ishmael (Father of the Arab nation), in Islam it is Ishmael—not Isaac—whom God asked Abraham to sacrifice.

By the Waters of the Sind

Black Water: The phrase came to be, and continues to be, synonymous with forced labor and life imprisonment. *Kalapani*, or black water, referred to the stretch of ocean between mainland India and colonial Britain's most notorious prison on the Andaman islands. To cross *kalapani* meant being condemned to permanent exile.

A Secular Comedy

One Sufi interpretation of the God/Satan myth portrays Satan (*Iblis*) as being in love with God, and thus the jealous lover when God asks him to bow to Adam. In his refusal to bow, he fulfills God's secret wish, for God is the Belovéd, and Satan the true monotheist. Satan says to God, "When You created me, you told me to bow to no one but You. Thus, I'm truer to Your word than You are." Hell is the absence of the Belovéd. (Evidence is now being discovered that Milton was familiar with this Sufi interpretation.)

Eleven Stars Over Andalusia

In the fall of 1993, I was sent a very literal version of this poem (called simply "Eleven Stars" in the Arabic) and asked to "convert it into poetry." Ahmad Dallal—who was then teaching at Smith College—went over that version with me, comparing it line by line with the Arabic original. As he did so, I took many notes and, some weeks later when I felt stymied, I decided to re-read Lorca (something that occurred to me because of the poem's reference to him). It was while reading Lorca that I found a way to tackle the task.

The phrase "eleven stars" comes directly from The Koran (Surah 12:4): "Joseph said to his father: 'Father, I dreamt of eleven stars and the sun and the moon; I saw them prostrate themselves before me.' 'My son,' he replied, 'say nothing of this dream to your brothers lest they plot evil against you.'"

CALL ME ISHMAEL TONIGHT

Differing from the Old Testament story of Abraham and Isaac, in The Koran the sacrifice is demanded not only of Abraham, but also of Ishmael. Directed by God, Abraham says to his son, Ishmael, "I see in a vision that I offer thee in sacrifice." Ishmael's willingness to be sacrificed heightens the beauty of God's redemption in which He says, "This is indeed a manifest trial."

Ghazals traditionally do not have titles, and most of these, in earlier or later versions, appeared simply as "Ghazal." For convenience, I have now titled most of them after their refrains.

Four ghazals that appeared in the collection of ghazals, *Call Me Ishmael Tonight,* are excluded to avoid duplication since they appeared in previous collections. Ghazals titled by the refrains "Even The Rain," "In Real Time," and "By Exiles" are simply titled "Ghazal" in *Rooms Are Never Finished*. The lattermost of these was written for Edward W. Said. The ghazal titled "Arabic" appears in *The Country Without a Post Office*.

An earlier version of "Tonight" is one of the ghazals in *The Country Without a Post Office*.

Agha Shahid Ali, a Kashmiri-American, was born on February 4, 1949, in New Delhi and grew up in Kashmir. He was educated at the University of Kashmir, Srinagar, and the University of Delhi. Shahid came to America in his early twenties and earned his Ph.D. at Pennsylvania State University in 1984 and his M.F.A. in Poetry at the University of Arizona in 1985. He taught at Hamilton College in New York, then became director of the M.F.A. Creative Writing program at the University of Massachusetts in Amherst. He also taught at the University of Utah and in the M.F.A. Program for Writers at Warren Wilson College. In the spring of 2000, Shahid was a visiting poet in the Graduate Creative Writing Program at N.Y.U. Agha Shahid Ali's volumes of poetry include *Bone-Sculpture* (1972), *In Memory of Begum Akhtar & Other Poems* (1979), *The Half-Inch Himalayas* (1987), *A Walk Through the Yellow Pages* (1987), *A Nostalgist's Map of America* (1991), *The Beloved Witness: Selected Poems* (1992), *The Country Without a Post Office* (1997), and *Rooms Are Never Finished* (2001). Shahid also translated Faiz Ahmed Faiz's collection *The Rebel's Silhouette: Selected Poems* and was the editor of *Ravishing DisUnities: Real Ghazals in English*. He was awarded Guggenheim and Ingram-Merrill fellowships and a Pushcart Prize, and his collection *Rooms Are Never Finished* was a finalist for the National Book Award in 2001. Agha Shahid Ali died on December 8, 2001.

INDEX

•